VOLKER "   L

Remember to
Walk the Talk

THE
digital
DEALERSHIP

A BATTLE-WORN ROADMAP TO ONLINE SUCCESS

DEDICATED

*To all automotive professionals, marketing departments
in dealer groups and OEM environment, owners of
dealerships, and all automotive peeps in the vendor world.*

&

*To my son Nicholas, who joined God's Army of Angels too
soon and is responsible for pushing me to do more with my
life, my vision, my goals, and my profession and to make
indeed a great career here in the U.S.*

*To my wonderful children, Denise, Nils, Eric, and
Pierre, and my loving spouse, Snowwhite, and
our expected baby, Max.*

*Last but not least to my parents, Gerhard and Anita
Jaeckel, who always believed that I could be successful
in life and my career in America so late in life.*

Acknowledgments

Sincere thanks to Wayne and Jeff Williams of Williams Auto World, who gave me the chance to start selling cars as a newbie with no experience at all.

I am super grateful to the car peeps and ex-bosses, GM Brian Mayfield at Nalley Volvo, Owner Harvey Jackson & Sales Director Slater Nalley at Jackson Acura, GM Lou Fantacone, GSM Kevin Fenner, GSM Arvind Sarathy, and GSM David Miles at Jim Ellis VW and Audi in Marietta, GA.

A huge "Thank You" to Clay Nalley, SONS Automotive Group, who trusted me to guide his dealerships successfully into the Digital Age.

Many thanks to Chris Reed from Cobalt for believing in me to advocate Digital Marketing and Social Media as his Digital Marketing Ambassador and Consumer Journey Visioneer.

Much appreciation to the Cobalt peeps, Charlie Buorton, Nicholas Villasenor, Nancy Haslett, Trisha Yount Burga, and Dennis Mosser, who assisted me to bring the gospel of the "Social Media for Breakfast" to their dealer clients and OEMs when everybody still thought social media was a fad.

I am grateful for knowing these car folks and marketing peeps: Joe Webb, Bill Playford, Kevin Frye, Tracy Myers, Tony Ly, Chris Fousek, Eric Miltsch, Jared Hamilton, Jody Devere, Anthony Bartoli, Tim W. Jackson, Yago Paramo, Brent Wees, Warren Austin, Bryan Armstrong, James Fabin, Paul Caldwell, Tom White Jr., JD Rucker, Joey Little, Ralph Paglia, Chris Hanson, and possibly 1000 more I can't all list on here. THANK YOU!

To Chad Parker, DDS, who helped me out when my tooth pain was killing me during writing and researching on an important chapter of this book. What a great dentist he is!

Contents

Introduction

When I came to the U.S., I hoped for Love, Life, and Freedom. Even so, I found that I had to overhaul my business experience and plans by 180 degrees.

After September 11 happened, I had only been in the U.S. for four weeks. I had been assigned by a German company to assist their American subsidiary and get it up and running, but it crumbled the same way the twin towers fell—into the ashes. I was officially out of work.

The Reinvention

Struggling to find a job (yes, not a career), I had only two things going for me: the extensive collection of sales and marketing books that I had brought over from Germany in two boxes, my suitcase of proper attire, and an accent. A lot of Americans liked my accent.

Even so, I did not want to start a library business with all those books, so I figured out that my German accent could be the gateway to a) making money and b) doing something with a product that I had loved since childhood—*cars*.

My marketing brain started spinning, and a light bulb went on. I was "stranded" in "Big Three Country"—a.k.a. Motor City—a small town an hour's drive west of Detroit named Mason. I was excited to see a car dealer on the outskirts of Michigan State University selling BMW, Mercedes-Benz, and Porsches to the citizens around Okemos, MI. The idea I had was to call this dealer up, ask for the owner, and tell him something.

And this is what I said.

"Mr. Williams, I think it would make sense to have a German guy, with a real German accent, selling your German cars."

It was a crazy idea. But a crazy idea that worked. It worked so well that I can now sit here and write those lines you have already read and hope you are continuing to read.

My Book

When I was featured in 2009 on the cover of the *Digital Dealer Magazine* in reflection of my unique way to approach digital marketing with having created early on in 2006/2007 social media presences as well as writing blogs for my dealership brands, the industry left and right, up and down the country seemed to recognize my unique approach and the early on adaption to convert prior traditional marketing in dealerships into new online and digital marketing dealerships and groups.

Through invitations to speak at conferences and receiving notice that I was considered as one of the top 10 ecommerce directors in 2009, this honor did not go unnoticed, and several industry vendors contacted me, offering me an array of positions, which would allow me to speak, write, and teach about my findings and approach on a national stage. In 2009 I joined Cobalt |ADP as their Digital Marketing Ambassador and started to teach and coach dealerships and OEMs with a new idea I had created: "The Social Media Breakfast for Champions."

As time went by and digital marketing evolved more—and acceptance in the industry was more open than ever—I was proud to work closely with Ford Direct and NADA as well as NCM 20-Groups.

I never pretended to know it all but taught, spoke, and coached about digital marketing, online car sales, and processes that I had established myself and proven to be successful in today's automotive Internet sales and digital marketing environment.

I am known for having walked the walk and not just talked the talk. I am known for turning companies around and making sales people successful, earning higher incomes than they had ever imagined.

I am coming out of the trenches after counter attacking broken processes and lethargic Internet sales departments throughout my career. Even though I am sometimes considered harsh and stubborn, I have the best in mind for your business and your success.

And that is essentially what this book is all about. Digital strategy is leaping forward, striking industries like lightning, and changing them forever. Keeping up with all these trends is nearly impossible, and it is twice as hard to implement them successfully the first time. Too many people fall for so-called experts in this digital marketing arena and hire somebody that they think must be top-notch only to find out later the people they spoke to and paid have not sold one car in their career.

I firmly believe that transforming yourself into a top selling digital strategist or helping your dealership understand these processes will accelerate your career and will make you the expert—the go-to guy. You need to focus on making car buying easier for your consumers by understanding how they think so that car selling is easier for your dealers. It is really that simple.

Yet this simplicity hides amidst a lot of bad information, outdated practices, and incorrect benchmarking. The savvy online marketing-oriented dealership always thinks ahead and is not afraid to test new processes to discover amazing data-sourced elements of truth for improved sales and customer satisfaction.

Welcome to your education on digital dealing. I promise that by the end, your mind will be buzzing with new ideas on how to improve the bottom line of your operation, cutting down on expenses, increasing customer loyalty, and—most important—having a dealer sales force that wants to be on your team.

Commander! Align your troops!

DRIVING CUSTOMER DATA FORWARD

CHAPTER 1

Embracing the New Customer Journey

"Never tell people how to do things. Tell them what to do and they will surprise you with their ingenuity."

GENERAL GEORGE PATTON

One of the very first things that you need to learn as an online marketing dealer is that your customer is central to every process that you ever need to implement. That means you have to start looking at them a lot more closely and caring about *how* they choose to buy a car.

This means honing in on driving customer data—which is exactly what your dealership needs to fully understand your key market segments. The very first step is properly defining the new customer journey.

Your Customer Journey Starts Now

Before any sale is made, there is a customer journey. This journey differs for everyone, but there is enormous value in understanding how your customers come to find, care about, and purchase from your dealership.

In the past, customer journeys were easy and simplistic. They would see your television or newspaper adverts; decide that they like you based on your advertising prevalence, pricing, or inventory; and buy a car. These days the Internet has brought a cascade of various media channels that your buyers use and engage with first before they decide to buy.

2003 - Becoming Digital

With no sales person vacancy open, Wayne Williams and his son Jeff loved my approach to ask for a job and allowed me to dip my toes into the car-selling circus. Starting out on the floor, traffic and demand for German luxury was challenging considering we were in Ford, Chrysler, and Chevy country. I had to find a way to gain opportunities despite being a lost lizard in Michigan's frigid winters.

In 2003 we saw a slight shift in "business as usual." We had regulars coming in and upgrading their 3-Series or ML-classes, and Mercedes-Benz started to reinvent their business approach from a majority in off-line marketing campaigns (print, TV, radio) into the online advertising arena.

Due to their efforts, we experienced an increase in so called "Star-Leads" (in affiliation with one of the most iconic brand logos in the world—the Mercedes-Benz Star) coming through the customer relations and lead management systems..

In those early days, there was no such thing as an Internet guy receiving these leads, and the sales manager solely received the leads from the OEM, gathered from several automotive web entities as well as their own Mercedes-Benz website. He printed these leads out and handed them to the veterans of the store.

The top dogs in the dealership, seasoned guys, who (according to them) sold cars since the wheel was invented in 3500 B.C., believed that these Star-Leads were not actually customers. Their reasoning was that "they always ask only for the best price", so the judgment was that these leads just could not be a real customer, because "How dare they not come to our dealership first?"

These "dinosaurs," a.k.a. seasoned sales guys, dropped the leads faster than a 150-year-old oak tree downtown from East Lansing during a tornado watch. When they finally dialed the prospect's phone number and caught a voicemail, no message was left for the inquiring customer! E-mail? "I don't send e-mails because I have no time for it." After just two to three days, the lead was marked as "not in the market," "lost customer," or something similar.

I know it is crazy! Seeing their cocky behavior and the frustration on my sales manager's face, I approached my manager as a green pea in this business and asked him to allow me to change the outcome of those leads. I knew that Mercedes-Benz was pressuring their dealers to be responsive and on the ball and to have a follow-up process for those leads in place.

He trusted my judgment, and I went ahead and adopted that typical German work ethic by planning a process and the follow-up —believing that it would bring a more positive outcome for the dealership. From that point, I received all these "known as not in the market" leads, re-opened those as "still in the market" customers, and created a schedule as well as a follow-up process on when to contact these inquiries, in what frequencies to touch the non-responding leads, what to send out via email or to say on the phone, and how to implement a unique selling proposition to show a differentiation between my dealership and the other dealerships fighting with me for the same customer.

In less than eight months of implementing my process, I quadrupled my sales numbers and ranked as the top dog among the older "sales pros" in our dealership. I also began to rank in the top-20 CSI (Customer Satisfaction Index) for the entire Midwest and Northeast for BMW sales consultants. Looks like Private Benjamin picked up the flag and protected it, just like South Carolinian Farmer Benjamin Martin during his heroic actions in the movie *The Patriot*.

Moving Forward With Digital Sales

This is the information age, and customers want as much information on and from you as they can get. Online marketing channels serve as the preferred locations where people find this information. This information can be obtained via email, by seeing paid search ads, visiting website, engaging in social media channels and referral traffic from blogs, and watching videos and other content-rich online entities.

The initial step of this customer journey places an additional element in front of the normal purchase funnel. That step is "awareness," which is becoming increasingly important to consumers of all ages and demographics.

The Road to Purchasing Online

The truth is that these customer paths are varied, and you almost never know how they are going to work for the individual. An eye-opening research from the Cobalt "Guide to the Modern Car Shopper"[1] shows that:

- Every day their entire online network generates 1.3 million leads.

- Each week five million visits are tracked to their website properties.

---

1   Tony Ly Cobalt, The Guide to the Modern Car Shopper eBook, http://www.slideshare.net/tonyly/cobalt-the-guide-to-the-modern-car-shopper-e-book-dec-4-2012

- Each month over a billion online ads are served to local shoppers and tracked by the brand.
- This results in a ½ billion inventory searches per year.

Based on this data, Cobalt deduced the following:

- The average car-shopping journey results in 19 hours of shopping, 60% of which is done online.
- While every journey is different, they all contain four phases.
  - *Inspiration:* Or brand awareness from ads and social media
  - *Discovery:* Research conducted by the shopper on manufacturer websites
  - *Engagement:* Contact initiation or a movement from online to real world contact
  - *Ownership:* Buyers create content and influence others

They are literally the last interaction your customer has before they decide to buy or not to buy from you. To have an opportunity to influence the prospects, you need to know that there are really only two types of interaction left : the interactions that assist with the purchasing decision and those that act as the last interaction before purchase.

A brand most likely will have lots of different touch points—a website, a blog, videos on YouTube, and a Facebook page, for a simple example. You need to create not only a multiple channel performance report using something such as Google Analytics but you should also consider "listening" in to the social sphere to find out how your customers are using each channel. A huge help for me was using free social monitoring tools like SocialMention, How Sociable, and TweetReach.

Best of all, once the data starts rolling in, you will be able to see which channels work best for your brand and customer outreach and engagement so that you can prioritize them for budget segmentation. Working with these tiered channels will expose you to whole audiences that you can access.

A well-organized, carefully-structured SEO strategy will complement any content or marketing goals that you plan on implementing there. Everyone's customer journeys are different, but the length of time it takes for a consumer to decide to buy is important.

Purchasing a car is one of the big life decisions. That is why you need to consider high value content and marketing strategies to sell to these "longer path" buyers.

What Is the Zero Moment of Truth?

Gone are the days of those long, leisurely family outings to shop around for a new car. People do not do that anymore because of busy schedules and long work hours, and—quite frankly—they have dealerships and brands available 24/7 with just the click of a mouse or a swipe on their smart phones and tablets. It has become rare that someone decides to buy a car and their next decision is to step onto your dealership show floor.

The marketing model has now shifted from "First Moment of Truth ," which was stepping onto the dealer lot, to the "Zero Moment of Truth"—or from random push advertising, impulse driven sales to a new way of pre-selective buying—the time after an ad impulse awakened the potential customer's interest in a product and before a purchase would be concluded.

In other words, the Zero Moment of Truth is that special time when consumers pop online to research your brand or product and to decide whether they want to continue to research and buy from you—or someone else. This shift has resulted in an upsurge in content production as companies fight to put out consistent, creative, and relevant content that educates and entertains their customers.[2]

---

2   What Is The Zero Moment of Truth?, http://www.teambishop.net/showcase/winning-the-zero-moment-of-truth-(zmot)/what-is-the-zero-moment-of-truth/297157

Why? Because it sells. The truth is that one in six car buyers[3] skips the test-drive, and nearly half visit just one (or no) dealership before they decide to purchase. What you put out there as content will help them to decide if they want to buy and if you are the right dealership to do business with.

Learning how to engage and win shoppers at the Zero Moment of Truth is a tried and true strategy that has helped me to gain market share and convince potential buyers to buy from me and my dealerships.

A Much-Needed Sales Funnel Debriefing

In the auto industry, the path to purchase is a lot more complicated than in most other industries due to the size of the asset you are trying to sell. These online shoppers that decide to buy from you before stepping into your showrooms are facing a host of different information, needs, and decisions before they arrive to the conclusion of whom to buy from.

You have to ask yourself as a digital marketing oriented dealer how your dealership can best attract, retain, and convert these virtual shoppers knowing that the automotive sales funnel is no longer a funnel. It can be any shape!

Dealers can buy into pre-selected lead programs helping them to predict when pre-qualified buyers will make their purchase with details like when, which vehicle, and how much they are willing to pay thrown into the mix.

New forms of lead generation are here, with data mining companies creating brutally accurate profiles of their customers, their behaviors, and their needs.

---

3   New Research: 1 in 6 Car Buyers Skip Test Drive; Nearly Half Visit Just One or No Dealership Prior to Purchase, http://www.prnewswire.com/news-releases/new-research-1-in-6-car-buyers-skips-test-drive-nearly-half-visit-just-one-or-no-dealership-prior-to-purchase-255302891.html

The knowledge obtained will give the online marketing oriented dealer the much needed insight into the consumer's use of mobile, social, and various forms of online aggregators. It will also show the tendency when shoppers are expected to visit your brick and mortar location.

This is why your sales funnel has become a lot more diluted but also a lot more opportunistic. Along with selling, you can use the various touch points to collect data that will improve your processes, methods, and dealership as a whole.

I remember that I never accepted any deal jacket from my sales people when there was not at least one email address noted. For us, as an Internet Sales department, it was an easy task considering that the incoming third party lead most likely had an email address. But what needs to happen is to have your entire corps of battle experienced sales people, and I am talking also of the floor sales personnel needed to follow the process, to get an email address from their customers when tailoring a deal for them.

The reason is so simple—consider the email as your life blood for the entire dealer organization in which all profit centers can benefit. Your finance and insurance department could send emails out when newer, better bank rates become available to save your customer a few more bucks.

The fixed operations can send email newsletters out informing customers about the "four tires and pay only for three" deals or that the sales department has the Susan G. Komen Drive for the Cure event coming up. Multiple touch points after the initial car sale has been made will keep your operations on top of the consumer's mind.

There is a reason for the proverb "out of sight, out of mind"; don't fall into this ambush.

ZMOT and the New Mental Model of Marketing

To drive the shift home for you, I am going to compare the old form of traditional marketing and the new form. You can see how an extra step has moved in to disrupt and improve the old mode of selling.

In the first, traditional marketing used to be a simple three-step process. In your customer's mind, first an advertisement or some kind of brand message would grab their attention and they would decide to visit your dealership; FMOT was born—the First Moment of Truth would happen at the dealership, your brick and mortar location.

This is when you handed them those keys for that test drive, haggled over the price, and introduced the potential customer to the service department and parts counter; it all contributed to their experience. Finally, the second moment of truth would happen—which is the eventual purchase decision. Based on your experience up until that point (brand messages, test drive, price, intro), the customer would decide to buy or not.

The new mental model of marketing[4] has an additional step—right between the initial stimulus and the first moment of truth. So the brand message grabs the buyer's attention, and their next decision is to perform pre-shopping research.

That can be done at home, work, vacation, or on their mobile without ever stopping into your store by utilizing your dealer website, manufacturer website, research websites, inventory websites, and, of course, reputation websites like Yelp, Dealerrater, Cars.com, Edmunds, and others. If they like what they see, the next step is to take their online experience and convert it into a real world experience. That is where the FMOT

---

4   ZMOT- The New Mental Model of Marketing, http://www.media-mosaic.com/blog/zmot/zmot-the-new-mental-model-of-marketing/

comes in again—and when your online content, telephone and/ or email responses, digital exposure, and impression have done their Mission Objective and you could convince your potential customer to visit you in your showroom.

From there it is up to you to provide the ideal in-store experience, which the consumer now certainly expects considering she was impressed already with your online demeanor. That means you need to provide excellent test drives and easy processes. If every checkpoint of your processes is going according to plan and your customer-perceived ZMOT experience is matching up with your FMOT, your customer will be more likely to enter into the second moment of truth and purchase.

This newer model of marketing is incredibly impactful, and it has given rise to new marketing entities, such as social media marketing, conversation marketing, and the marketer's favorite buzz word—content marketing. Consider these forms of Marketing 3.0 now a part of your advanced "digital strategy."

Speaking of Marketing 3.0, your dealership needs to adjust the current executed marketing. As it is for everything new on the horizon, the challenge is to make this implementation as smooth as possible, and even though you need to do it *now*, keep in mind "Rome was not built in one day."

See it like you have just enjoyed the birth of your new baby; everything is new for you and your spouse. From changing diapers to feeding and playing, this task not only requires patience but also sets you up to endure the habit of persistence. Like your baby, you need to consider this time of implementation of a process with the Crawl – Walk – Run approach. Before any baby will ever walk, it has to go through the "school" of crawling first, reaching the couch or table, pulling herself up on it to reach for grandma's crystal vase.... Like the baby, you and your process implementation will experience some bumps and bruises before you are off and running. It will happen—guaranteed. —with time, determination, and a "never give up" attitude!

Now get out there and brief your troops again on the sales funnel you had followed all these years, and inform them that tactical changes are coming and that you will master them.

Automotive Study Results: Your New Mandate

The automotive study that Google conducted is very illuminating. Take a look at this eye-opening research data that indicate how important it is to begin your Marketing 3.0 mandate as soon as possible.

- In the auto industry, it takes people anywhere between one month to a year to decide to buy a car. The most common time is two to three months, as I mentioned earlier. That implies that you need to start consistently producing new and engaging content on your web entities as well as your social media engagement to facilitate this long-term ZMOT process.

- Google also discovered that car shoppers use an average of 18.2 sources of information to help them decide where to buy. Even more shocking is that for any single source, some 34% of shoppers are using it. That makes allying yourself with large industry blogs, car sales websites and social accounts high priority so you would be the part of the Stimulus shoppers endure online.

- The research also shows that people rely on ZMOT information just as much as they rely on FMOT information. The two are equal. This implies that ZMOT may become the more influential sales funnel element to focus on in the future. If you lose a customer during this point of market entry, he or she will most likely never make it to your dealership floor.

- Many of the most influential sources of information come from online use. Website quote requests come in at 59%, comparison shopping comes in at 45%, and dealership inventory comes in at 44%.[5] These are stats that will help you streamline your online and offline marketing approach.

- One of the main reasons why auto shoppers look online is to check availability (they like shopping somewhere close) and to express their individuality by building a vehicle they love. This indicates that your geo-location based marketing practices need to be improved along with the integration of custom web content generation.

It is now up to you to build a cohesive ZMOT and FMOT process. We know that after the achievement of having sold the car to your customers, the aftermath of the purchase is just as important as it was to get the customer to your location. New customers love to engage with their friends, peeps, and peers after the purchase. They are taking pics of their new ride, share it on social networks, or even create blog posts. This user-generated content is a welcome opportunity for you to nourish the relations with your customers, and you may even use it for your internal content creation for newsletters, customer appreciation days, etc.—just make sure you have a written consent form signed by your customer allowing you to use their picture and/or share their "A"-rated experience.

Keep in mind that when your potential customers experience any major discrepancy during the initial contact and selling approach, widely known also as Bait and Switch, this idea of ZMOT meets FMOT will fire back. Make sure that inconsistency in your designed process will not bite you in the backside and fail the MO (mission objective).

---

5   Google Shopper Sciences, Zero Moment of Truth Study, Automotive, 2011

CHAPTER 2

Selling With Generational Variances

"It doesn't take a hero to order men into battle. It takes a hero to be one of those men who goes into battle."

NORMAN SCHWARZKOP

With the rise and awareness of ZMOT and the shifts in the market that have occurred, it has become necessary to target customer segments for increased sales.

Generational variances are extremely important because you cannot sell the same way to people from different generations. They simply do not respond like that. Let's take a close look at how customer segments and online targeting are used today.

Customer Segments and Online Targeting

In every niche, customer targeting has been important over the years for salesmen within the car profession. With the advent of the Internet, online marketing, and the reign of ZMOT, it has become possible to divide your target customers into segments so that you can better understand them as people, their needs, and what to accomplish with their new purchase.

Customer segmenting is about dividing your customers into groups—by demographic, behavior, benefits, age, or location. Identify the segments, and use portions of your online marketing on those groups of people for selective and targeted marketing messages.

Selling to Baby Boomers: The Facts

Considering the moment in time, at the very top of your list should be baby boomers. This customer segment is divided by age—or more correctly, people born in the 1950s and '60s. People that are older than 50 currently count for 62.3%[6] of the auto retail market.

Additional research pointed out further is that baby boomers are the people that are spending the most money on cars. They out-bought the millennial generation by millions of cars a few short years ago. The interesting thing is that even though baby boomers tend to buy new cars a lot more often, most car manufacturers are focused on selling to the younger generations.

If you are a digital marketing strategist like I am, you instantly understand the opportunity. Instead of car sales declining with age, they increase—which means that for many dealerships, the most lucrative market segment should indeed be these boomers.

According to the University of Michigan's Transportation Research Institute, the 55- to 64-year-old age group is the most likely segment to buy a new car. Just a few years ago this was not the case, but markets can be surprising—as long as you keep your eyes on the data.

---

6   Sharon Silke Carty, Auto Sales Driven by Boomers, Automakers Desperate for Millennial Love, http://www.huffingtonpost.com/2012/05/04/baby-boomers-driving-cars_n_1475243.html

Baby boomers do not want to retire and disappear from consumerism—they want to stay as young as they can, for as long as they can. This often means buying a new ride, no matter if new or used. These empty nesters finally can buy the desired two-seater convertible they craved all those years while the kids were growing up, finishing college, spreading their wings until they (finally) left home. Not surprising—some boomers get a new car every year. They can afford it and want to catch up on the "dreams" they had put on hold, such as driving a Corvette or a Mazda Miata with their soul mate on Route 66.

Do your research. Ask your OEM-Rep. for data she may have on the DMA. Are there any indications that you live in an area known for a higher number than usual two-person households? What are the age brackets of the population in your dealership's vicinity?

Spend a couple of hours around the closest mall, and take a look what cars are parked there. Who else other than new moms with their newborns are there in the morning roaming the hallways? What I want to say is to be more aware of your surroundings; look around at local diners, hardware stores, and so on. You will be amazed how a little open eye observation can account for new creative ideas.

With our MINI dealership, for example, the OEM was thinking that we would have way more millennials approaching our inventory and suggested an 80/20 order status on models with manual transmission (80% to 20% automatic transmission). The real world could not have been much different. It actually turned out that 60% of our sold MINIs were purchased by baby boomers (and older) in the first year, with the majority deciding on automatic transmissions. Based on the fact that the Southern part of Atlanta and the surrounding were communities of two-person households and retirees, who wanted to relive the shagadelic times of the late '60s and the epoch when the MINI was *the* car to have, hip arthritis-baffled bodies of these customers just wanted to glide with the 5-speed automatic transmission instead of quirking around a 6-speed manual during the stop-and-go traffic nightmare of Atlanta. So much for "knowing your data, your DMA, and your customer."

Selling to Generation X: Revelations

Generation X, or kids of the '70s, are the people who were born after the World War II baby boom. They are typically aged between 30 and 49, and they have a real place in the market. As more and more baby boomers retire, it is the Gen Xers that will step into the "big jobs."

They currently make up a sizable 36% of the workforce,[7] so they are an inbuilt generation of people that will buy cars. Targeting them will lead to revelations about your dealership because Xers are part of a generation that love innovative, new experiences and great customer service.

Plus, they are the generation most influencing the younger Gen Ys. These are the parents, bosses, teachers, and professors.-For Generation X, you can get a little more creative with your selling approach, involving things such as advanced social selling. These individuals do their research, and they want to know that you have a sound service model when they step through your doors.

I want to especially stress the "Customer Service" aspect. The Gen X parents, for example, have one particular thing they all lack, and this is *time*. This deficiency of time comes from the duties that are evolving around them being younger parents. We all know someone in our circle of friends and acquaintances who it seems constantly is on the run, meaning Monday afternoon bringing

---

7   Shannon Neeser, The Unsung Generation: How Xers Add Value to Your Association, http://xyzuniversity.com/2014/01/the-unsung-generation-how-xers-add-value-to-your-association/

little Josh to Little League practice and when finished, rushing downtown to pick up Kendra from ballet. Then they head home, letting the dog out and quickly buying the forgotten pasta sauce for that night's dinner. And wait, that was only Monday...so you see what I meant that these Gen Xers need great customer service.

For you as an Internet sales person, trying to answer your Gen X parents' request for a quote is now the time to shine. When you sense that this potential customer is a Gen Xer, offer to bring the car to the location they choose and take a test-drive when the family is in their comfortable environment. When discussing maintenance, offer them a pick-up–drop-off service with a porter dropping off a loaner car and taking their car back to the dealership to get serviced.

When I worked for Schumacher Mercedes-Benz in Arizona, I had a 30-year-old mother stop by at the dealership. Her interest was a C230 Sport, as she had mentioned earlier on the phone. She also mentioned that she could only be a maximum of one hour at the dealership, including the test-drive and talking numbers, due to coming with her newborn and the need to pick up her other son from school later on. With a set time of her being at the dealership, I pulled the car out of the line-up, let the AC run, and put a bottle of ice cold water in the cup holder; I did all of these things ahead the time.

When she arrived, I offered to have my assistant look after the sleeping newborn in my well-climated office. Long story short, she loved the car, loved the fact that the inside of the car was cooled perfectly in Arizona's 103 degrees outside temperature, and thought the chilled water in the cup holder tasted like a million bucks.

During selection of a desired color and walking the lot, I carried the booster seat of the little one the entire time, and even when we closed the deal and I walked her down to the F&I office, I made sure she did not have to carry the baby in the heat.

This Gen X mom gave us raving reviews, and my personal CSI was pointing out "that the sales person provided a service that was not found at any other three Mercedes-Benz dealerships in the Valley" and that carrying the baby the entire time put her at ease and made her feel that we were totally focused on her and the task she wanted to accomplish. Even so, the price was not the lowest; it was the courtesy and service she experienced that made her *want* to buy the car there.

Selling to Generation Y: The Intelligence Market

And then there is Generation Y. They are the tech generation, the ones that grew up with advanced technology and social media, and they are developing everything from robotic prosthetics to augmented reality TV games.

Yet for such a progressive generation, they do not buy many cars. These guys were born between 1982 and 1995, and generally speaking, they do not buy much of anything.[8] This is because they hate "hard" selling methods and prefer advice over pushy marketing messages. They want intelligence, ethics, and environmentally-friendly brands—not sharks.

This generation refuses to respond to incompetent brands. Incompetency in their eyes ranges from the inability to sell ethically to a brand not having a full online presence. They judge you based on that!

And still Gen Ys are the wealthiest generation by far—with a projected annual income of $3.8 trillion by 2018.[9] If you are going to target anyone, it makes sense to target this segment. But it is by far the hardest segment to target; even so, these millennials

---

8   Sarah Sladek, Why Gen Y Won't Buy What You're Selling, http://xyzuniversity. com/2012/10/why-gen-y-wont-buy-what-youre-selling/

9   Next Generation Car Buyer Study, http://www.autonews.com/assets/PDF/ CA90353823.PDF

are on pace (according to a J.D. Power study "Gen Y") to increase their 2014 car purchases by 16 percent compared to 2013.

Generation Ys are completely impervious to old school marketing tactics; they ignore traditional advertising and by far prefer up-and-coming efforts, like viral videos, social media, apps, integrated media, brand mashups, and fun, entertaining events.

The only way to sell cars to Gen Ys is to adhere to their philosophy. Their purchases need to be worth it, empowering, and able to connect people. Associating yourself with causes is also incredibly important.

Keep in mind that Generation Ys grew up in a highly competitive, technologically capable and ego-driven world. They are very loyal brand advocates as long as you stay on the path and are ethical about doing business or making sales.

The Next Gen Car Buyer: What Millennials Want

The truth is that millennials want something that is fairly straightforward; it is just harder for marketers than the old type of selling. The good news is that this creates a lot of opportunities for digital strategists willing to take risks and pay their dues with research and data.

Here are some critical industry points that you need to understand about marketing cars to millennials.

- Younger millennials are not getting their driver's licenses as quickly. The reasons cited have been that they are too busy with other things (23%), they want more time to train (14%), they are afraid of driving (19%), and it is too expensive (15%).[10]
- The bottom line is that research indicates that half of all

---

10   Next Generation Car Buyer Study, http://www.autonews.com/assets/PDF/CA90353823.PDF

younger millennials and 16% of older millennials do not own a vehicle because of cost. They find it too expensive.

- Millennials like to purchase cars that say something about who they are. This means buying a vehicle from a brand that aligns with their self-image.

To market to this customer segment, you will need to focus on word-of-mouth marketing, which means face-to-face, unique content creation, forum, and recommendations and reviews from other buyers.

Selling to Generation Z: Acceleration

There is a new generation in town, and they are quickly becoming a key market segment as they get older. Generation Zs were born between 1996 and 2009, and they are fierce, competitive, and highly connected.

They are already influencing what their parents buy, and soon they will be old enough to drive cars. When this happens, expect them to demand even more information, transparency, high quality service, and impressive brand campaigns.

Studies are already being conducted into the "partial attention" span that this generation has grown up with. They are permanently attached to their phones, are constantly connected to hundreds of other people, and form a virtually impenetrable barrier for dealers that do not take the time to prepare for their arrival.

- This generation will demand more integrated technologies and digital strategies that unite both the online world and the real world. Think wearable technology and various channels working together to form a brand message.
- Generation Z will also shop with a brighter conscience, which means that they want to know exactly how your

dealership runs before they buy from you. You will have to be their friend before you are their car brand.

- Their aspirations will be similar to their Gen Y parents in that they will value advanced technology, new innovations, real time relevance, and clever strategy to become interested in a brand.

- In the future, dealerships may have to change their in-store structures[11] to integrate more seamlessly with new technologies that can reach these markets.

BMW, for example, has started to include BMW Geniuses[12] into their sales process. With digital flat screen displays and showroom technology, product geniuses are the new floor salesmen. These people can explain the amazing technology behind the vehicles to potential buyers.

Many of these urban stores[13] will begin to integrate the online space into the showrooms for a seamless online–offline buying experience. This will give brands virtually unlimited retail space thanks to digital tools like an interactive powerwall configurator.

Like their parents,[14] they will prefer practical cars that fit into their current lifestyles—opting for relevant vehicles instead of flashy, overpriced ones. Your marketing strategies will have to include a lot of data on this segment so that you can prepare for their market onslaught.

---

11   Gen Z Shopping: Designing Retail for the Constant State of Partial Attention, http://www.fitch.com/content/uploads/2013/09/GenZshopping_09_09_13_final.pdf

12   Christina Rogers, BMW Tosses Salesmen for 'Geniuses,' http://online.wsj.com/news/articles/SB10001424052702304450904579364833799765354

13   Sarwant Singh, The Future of Car Retailing, http://www.forbes.com/sites/sarwantsingh/2014/02/05/the-future-of-car-retailing/

14   Gen X Prefers Practical Cars, http://www.autotrader.com/research/article/car-news/109798/gen-x-prefers-practical-cars.jsp

section 2

DRIVING TEAM DYNAMICS FOR COLLABORATIVE SALES

CHAPTER 3

Assembling Your "Special-Ops" Team

"I am more afraid of an army of 100 sheep led by a lion than an army of 100 lions led by a sheep."

TALLEYRAND

s an ex-military police staff sergeant for the German Armed Forces, a lot of the presentations and strategies that I present involve military and battle analogies. I discovered that leadership, team building, relying on your team and each other, strategy, and conquering tasks have a lot in common with the education and discipline I have encountered thorough my career as a soldier. When you are convinced and dedicated to the cause, your operation, and the goals you want to achieve during your daily battle, the core values are a necessity.

A combat strategy is similar to our online marketing world's strategy. Digital strategy does not have to be difficult if you focus on creating the right framework first. One of the main components for any battalion or (for our purpose here) car dealership will be the team you build. Any work that gets done must be handled by reliable experts in their fields that collaborate like a Band of Brothers would do.

How to Build Your Automotive Sales Team

I have created some key rules for building my digital operations sales team that I believe will bring your dealership an advantage in the market you are operating in:

- Pick your team wisely. Your soldiers need to be able to function together and collaborate on complex tasks, have each other's back, and fit into the business culture that you have established while having the freedom to lead your dealership in new marketing directions.

- Focus on a diverse, tested team. You as the Ecommerce Guy are the captain. Now your "special-ops team" needs a specialist like a techie person, who knows how to set up some landing pages and would be comfortable with some coding in case you have more than five dealerships. Get one or two ISMs (Internet Sales Managers) in place, who will assist you to control and guide these ISPs (Internet Sales Persons). When your business structure allows, think about widening the special ops like adding Business Development Center people in, who will assist your profit centers like service and parts departments.

- Set evaluation timelines. Each of your team members needs to prove their worth in your digital strategy team. Everything needs to be grounded in data and proved with adequate reporting and metrics analysis.

Your digital teams will not only focus on selling more vehicles but will carry the flag of your entire online marketing strategy. They will show that your vision was the right one and that the processes you integrated are working, and I can guarantee that by distributing different tasks to different specialists in your corps, everybody will know exactly what the mission's goal is.

Harvard Business Review defines digital teams as the people responsible for "developing, testing and implementing a strategy to reach and engage target audiences through digital channels."[15]

Headlights on Leader Selection

Digital skills are uncommon, but they are also attracting a lot of new players in the field. That means to find team members that can actually do their jobs well, you need to hire a leader first. Aside from you as the head digital strategist, your ISM will help you hire, manage teams, and execute strategy.

Your new Ecommerce Director is your digital strategy project leader and should be the person that pioneers online targeting and Internet sales for your dealership, so aim high. They need to have the following criteria:

- At least six or more years working in the automotive digital and online marketing strategy, with acumen working with diverse team members, vendors, and the dealership's other profit centers. Also, I would strongly encourage you to look for candidates that actually have sold cars successfully themselves and know what the "daily grind" really means before sitting them in the captain's chair. I see it like this: Would you let someone perform an open heart surgery on you knowing that he got all his knowledge from WebMD and some YouTube videos? The real world mix and prior lived situations makes the outcome!

- Ask for proven metrics. What data can they show you where they have achieved success with past campaigns? What have

---

15   Perry Hewitt, How to Build a High-Performing Digital Team, http://blogs.hbr.org/2013/08/how-to-build-a-high-performing/

they focused their attention on? What metrics are they good at establishing and getting a return on? Ask these questions.

- Sit your new digital leader down and ask them what their work ethic is like and what their strategic planning process focuses on. I remember a meeting in which an auto group Ecom & Marketing Director told me that he only works Monday to Friday from 8 a.m. to 5 p.m.; after that time he closes down his laptop. I was shocked! How about you? Their answer will reveal a lot about their experience and who they are as people.

- I would encourage you to pose hypothetical strategy questions to this individual to see if they have the creativity required to sell in this new way.

- Make sure that your new digital strategist is able to work with your entire sales team. The reason is that there will be friction at some point, where floor sales people—let's put it politely—"dislike" the digital team. So will the sales manager. I saw over all these years that commitments were made by owners and "full backing" of the new digital sales approach and online marketing was encouraged, but the first guys to intervene with the new approach were the sales managers. Believe me, it will happen!

Turn your headlights on leader selection in the right way, and you will find an individual that will help you facilitate all of your digital strategies. That means you can delegate marketing tasks to their team while still being able to focus on your dealership operations.

Great digital dealers are inventive,[16] they help bring people together, and they have the ability to empathize with all of their

---

16   Jeremiah Handrick, What Makes for a Great Digital Strategist, http://jeremiahandrick.com/notes/2012/03/19/what-makes-for-a-great-digital-strategist

team members. Most of all, they have good ideas. If you are the main strategist, that is fine, but then fill the role. If you do not have time, hire a second "leader" to deal with the more technical side of digital strategy.

Creating Clear Team Hierarchies

One of the main reasons teams do not function well together is that they do not understand how they fit together as a team. This includes detailing what their roles are inside your team, what is expected of them, and who they should report to in a traditional hierarchy.

Want proof of that? Take a look:

I do not understand department leaders, in this case, an ecommerce director of a three franchise high-line store, allowing an Internet salesperson to call him "dude" in front of newly hired Internet sales people with almost every sentence exchanged. What does the ecom director do? Nothing! Ask yourself right now what that does to the morale of the group he is leading. Do you think he appears as a strong leader, who, when he gives orders like "Let's do a 75 phone call follow-up" everybody screams "Hooray" and begins right away, or is it more likely that the sales people will try to negotiate with their "dude" that 50 phone calls are enough?

You make the call—I already did and will hold it like this George Washington once said: "Be courteous to all, but intimate with few; and let those few be well-tried before you give them your confidence."

There are three stages that are involved in creating creative hierarchies for sound operations. If you structure these correctly, they will result in teams that are able to make coherent decisions and get things done on time.

The first level is called annotation.[17] During this phase, you need to get your team together to begin working on a project—if that was now, the creative wording for your next outbound email campaign or the next customer appreciation day cook-out for all of your open online inquiries. They will expose many issues right off by engaging with each other and making basic mistakes.

You will need to establish a way for your team members to share their ideas, get clear feedback, and centralize that feedback for all to see. This means exploring the team infrastructure and giving everyone their accurate place in the team.

From there you will move to the second level: The Workflow, which is the process of removing those initial mistakes and establishing proper systems for creating, approving, and completing work. There needs to be levels of authority and someone that always has the final say. And this someone should be the Ecom Director or Internet Sales Director.

When you work with an outside vendor together, like an ad agency that has handled your offline marketing approach, make sure you are on the same page, which means mirroring the traditional campaigns with your online approach or vice versa.

Once the workflows have been tested and sorted out, your team can move on to the third level of Creative Operations, where you will implement the business intelligence structures that will improve your team's performance over time.

This means benchmarking progress and establishing metrics to measure so that improvements can be made to all processes and flows. The extras, like allocation of resources and projected team growth, can be sorted out as you implement strategy.

A good team hierarchy works like a well-oiled machine because everyone is orientated and knows exactly who to report to and what

---

17   The Hierarchy of Work-In-Progress Strategies, http://www.conceptshare. com/2014/04/the-hierarchy-of-work-in-progress-strategies/

they are meant to do with their time. This makes great decision making easier and leads to faster project implementation and rewards.

What Doesn't Kill Us Makes Us Tougher

I worked for Volvo as their new selling and managing Internet Sales Director. The two Internet managers who I inherited did not want to follow the processes I had put in place to handle those incoming Internet leads as well as already received Internet leads for a long-term follow up for 90+ days.

They had two options: 1. Follow the process and be successful or 2. Leave the Internet department and get back on the floor. For people who have sold Volvo in the time they were dropped by Ford and offered for sale to an Indian company, they possibly know already that it was not an easy task to sell the Swedish cars with a dated product pallet, especially as a floor sales person with the shortcomings of floor traffic.

They decided to leave the next day the—not the Internet department but the company. They clearly wanted me to fail as a leader with an attitude of "Do your [blank] alone. Good luck."

When the going gets tough, the tough get going.

Similar to efforts in joining the Navy Seals, you are never short of an array of applicants. The only difference is that through their so-called "Hell Week," not everybody will qualify to join this elite group in the end. Numbers are up; around one in six will make it. The training is purposefully hard, exhausting, and designed to make most people fail. Navy Seals want to have the best staff, who are persistent, do not give up, have their goal in mind to succeed, and want to be the best.

And this is where a well-functioning Internet department comes in. Not everybody is "designed" to be an Internet guy or gal. The two Internet managers who left wanted to be "Navy Seals," but they were playing as battle re-enacters and not real soldiers.

As a leader, when you see that somebody is not willing to give it their all, and all-coaching methods you had put in place just signaled "riot" and insubordination to undermine your efforts as a leader, tell that person to find a job elsewhere in the company but not in your fighter group.

Leveraging Team Skills to Get the Job Done

Aside from a lack of time, the second largest issue with digital brand teams is that there is a lack of skill within the existing teams that the ecommerce director has assembled. This is going to cause untold strife as you try to move forward with your strategies.

Much like any battle scenario, if a single team member does not hold their own, it creates gaps in the front line. Approaches, tactics, and strategies fail when team members cannot or do not know how to fulfill their role correctly. This is why hiring the correct team is so essential to the end result of all of your projected digital strategies.

- Your team needs to work closely together to get the job done. That means you need to make sure that each member's skills complements the others and that there is a good mix of strengths and weaknesses to balance team dynamics well. If not, holes will begin to appear, and certain team members will be left behind.

- To leverage these unique team skills, you also have to consider personality clashes as these will interfere with strategy time and time again. In your working environment, if one team member does not like another or there is serious dissention among your troops, you will not be able to launch a united front with your campaigns.

Realistically, this means that your team will only function efficiently once they are all on the same page, pulling for the same results, and working towards a single goal. Great teams identify more opportunities, work better together, and achieve more success than others.

Finding Talent from within

Of course, being two men short and I as the one-man department, I had to find talent—a good person that was not tainted yet from other Internet departments that they had experienced in their former car career. I needed to find at least one person that needed guidance, wanted to be the best, and wanted to follow processes mapped out from day one to day ninety so that they could use it as "what do I have to do now?"

When looking at the current staff employed by this Volvo dealership, one guy jumped out. He was new (11 weeks on board), tried hard, but just did not sell more than three to four cars in a month—even though eight was the minimum to keep your job in the organization. He was a real estate agent and left his job due to the bursting housing bubble, and one thing what stuck out to me was that he had a great voice on the phone.

He tried hard, but he was always short and would soon get kicked out due to lack of sales by the GSM. As the clock was ticking down towards the last day of the month—with three cars sold—I went to my General Sales Manager and asked him if he would be willing to give him to me to join the current one-man Internet department, and he agreed.

Long story short: After two months this gentleman sold 14 cars! Combined with my efforts and the processes I had included to "really take care of business and customers," our two-man department generated an average of 36 to 40 car sales. Volvos!

We went through training, utilized his very soothing phone voice to set appointments, and the female customers loved it. We followed up on "lost leads" only to find that 60 percent were still in the market for buying a car, worked long hours (that is what it takes to make it on your own and succeed), and started new and fresh with zero cars sold on the first day of the month.

Considering that our entire store sold between 110–120 cars total—with eight floor sales people and two Internet guys—I guess he and I went through "Hell Week" camp and earned our Seal Trident.

Why Trust Is Good but Control Is Better

We Germans have an old saying: "Trust is good but control is better." In the virtual world of metrics, analytics, and accountability, this nugget can save you a lot of time and effort. There are so many variables involved in leading a team-that it can be hard to trust a new team that barely has any real procedures or policies to work with.

It is important to trust your team with their tasks to reach clients via outbound phone calls, the numbers of upcoming appointments, and following your implemented follow-up process, but it is ignorant to believe that they will somehow spring together and work together seamlessly without any control.

Your job will be to facilitate your team interactions, to establish structures and hierarchies, and then to focus on what matters—building strategies and, even more important, selling more cars as a result of your efforts. The three limitations of this are time, resources, and money. These need to be carefully mapped out so that you can orientate your team and your superiors when ideas and brainstorming begin.

I have seen very promising teams put together, and then—due to lack of structure and management—they have failed in their first few campaigns.

Once you have done all of this basic groundwork,[18] it can move from control to trust. Then you can go to conferences, events, and daily meetings while your team stays behind and does their work successfully. They should be able to get vast volumes of your strategy work done for you while you are away.

A Culture of Innate Experience Cycles

I have a philosophy with digital teams that has served me well throughout the last decade worth of experience. All teams are different and have their own unique challenges—and each time you establish one, you have to start from the ground up.

All competent ecommerce guys and gals need to treat their teams like newborns. First you learn to crawl, then walk, then run. There is no other process that works better in digital strategy. Once you have gone through crawling, walking, and running, you do it all over again.

This establishes a culture of "experience cycles" inside your online team. It is okay to make mistakes as long as they are acknowledged, measured, analyzed, and fixed in the next cycle.

When a team is not afraid to test new endeavors, they complete these cycles faster, which also improves your chances of getting more results in and more insights from that data. With every experience cycle that runs, your team will get to know what works and what does not work with your audience and your dealership.

That is why you need to foster a culture of experience cycles in your team—whether you are only three people or 30. The term "experience cycle" comes from the process of gaining experience each time you implement a strategy or test a tactic.

---

18   Amanda Shaw, How to Take Control of Your Digital Marketing, http://webrunnermedia.com/control-your-digital-marketing/

As all digital teams come to discover, digital strategy is more than simply choosing a suite of programs and platforms[19]; it is what you do with these over time that counts. This will take hundreds of cycles and months of continuous testing and reapplication.

The digital arena is never something you can do once and leave alone. It is not ever the set-it-and-forget-it rotisserie chicken grill mentality. It takes constant time and reanalysis—and a hunger for achieving greater results with fewer overheads. This culture must pervade your team, and each of them should be just as hungry as you are to test and improve the strategies and tactics that you implement.

---

19   Organizing for Digital Success, http://razorfishoutlook.razorfish.com/articles/organizingdigital.aspx#01

CHAPTER 4

The Nature of Driving Team Sales Collaboration

"Victorious warriors win first and then go to war, while defeated warriors go to war first and then seek to win."

SUN TZU, THE ART OF WAR

t is not enough to assemble a great team that is poised for combat on the digital battlefield; you also need to understand how these teams connect, collaborate, and are directly responsible for the results of your chosen online strategy.

According to Digital Strategy Consulting, some 47%[20] of people have identified "lack of time" as the top barrier to better customer analytics. This is interesting because a functional team that has been assembled correctly should never fall short of time. It seems that there is a bug in their strategic planning.

---

20   Digital Marketing Blocked by Skills and Time in Brand Teams, http://www.digitalstrategyconsulting.com/intelligence/2014/02/most_digital_marketers_expect_a_single_view_of_the_customer_by_2016_infographic.php

The Lonely Scout Analogy

With digital strategy management being so critical to success,[21] effective long-term strategies need to come from trained, collaborative teams. In military operations and strategic training, one of the first things that you are taught is to trust the team member next to you. They will have your back when bullets start flying and people start dying.

I like to illustrate this point using the lonely scout analogy. Scouts that are sent into war zones without backup are often KIA. That is why they usually pair them in twos or group them in tactical teams—to reduce casualty numbers. It is the same with your digital automotive strategy team.

Placing an enormous amount of responsibility on one team member because the others are still learning or are not holding their own changes the dynamic. What ends up happening is that they become overwhelmed and cannot maintain their part on the strategy. It fails. It takes a whole team of people to successfully execute a digital strategy.

If you want to sell more cars, more often, you need to realize that it is your team that does it as a whole unit and not one particularly talented digital marketer, SEO guy, or Ecom Director. You might have the world's greatest SEO specialist, so lots of inbound traffic arrives to your website, but if your other team members have not prepared to address these leads in the form of increased phone calls and/or email inquiries, you are looking at a lot of dead traffic and no conversions at all. Do not force your team members to be lonely scouts on the battlefield. It might look like it works for a while, but ultimately, it will fail miserably due to the lack of cohesiveness. Make sure that your team is a balanced unit.

---

21   Analysts Say Digital Strategy Management Is Critical To Success, http://aptris. com/news-events/itsm-insights/itsm/analysts-say-digital-strategy-management-is-critical-to-success/

The latest Forrester Research report on "The State of Digital Business in 2014" underlines the words written above. Even though 74%[22] of companies say that they have a digital strategy, only 15% feel confident enough to execute a complete strategy in their market. That is a massive disconnect.

Build Accountability Into Team Dynamics

Another concern that many digital strategists are experiencing right now in the automotive industry is the widespread lack of accountability with their teams and strategies.

In digital strategy, as in the military, each person needs be responsible for their performance based on their job description, the parameters they work in, and the objectives that they need to meet.

In this age of metrics and data analysis, it is a necessity to compile reports on progress from each individual member of your team. This is one way of building accountability into your team dynamics. Focus on establishing a big data system and a reporting process. Early on, I provided for my team reports by showing how the individuals acted on leads received and chats responded to; handled phone calls, emails, and initial lead responses answered; appointment show ratios; set appointments; etc. All of these key performance indicators were measured on ratios as well as time spent on them.

In order for the team to not get lost in the amount of numbers, lines, and data, early on in 2006 we developed the kind of ample system signalizing the ISM's array of cell content in the spreadsheet. Red cell content – You are behind the pace; watch it; it has to improve! Yellow was more like caution; you are still

---

22   Paul Krill, Forrester: Businesses Having Trouble Getting With the Digital Times, http://www.infoworld.com/t/it-strategy/forrester-businesses-having-trouble-getting-the-digital-times-241997

away from your objectives and could slide into red. And green signalized – You are doing your job! You are right on the money!

Steve Parker[23] once said that "people" are the only apps for digital strategy and accountability. Each individual team member needs to understand their "why" and has to know how to justify their decisions. They are accountable, and this is the real world. Otherwise, the "not doing" will start to thin out marketing money, skill development, and positive results.

You, as the lead digital strategist, need to devise a method of building accountability in your team dynamics. It is up to you, the Ecom Director or department head, to establish these KPIs. Be reasonable when laying down the land.

Defending Your Digital Marketing Deployment

In case you did not realize it yet, your automotive online team is a marketing department all on its own. As all marketing departments are responsible for budgets, how they are spent, and what kind of returns the company is getting, your team will be no different. Accountability begins at the point where you start really dealing with the numbers.

- **Own it.** Every dealership, even when they have the same brands on the lot as you do, is different, and so is every Internet team. You probably will not use the same strategies that other dealerships and their teams use. That means that you need to own the decisions that you have made.

- **Defend it.** Institute a method for metric analysis that is going to make justifying your strategies easier with the company leadership. Stats and charts are a necessity to

---

23   Steve Parker, Lack of Digital Strategy & Accountability Is Killing Brands, http://blogs.imediaconnection.com/blog/2012/03/01/lack-of-digital-strategy-accountability-is-killing-brands/

achieve a certain company goal. Securing your future online marketing budgets and strategic digital moves should come from a unified team that believes in what they can achieve and that can be backed up with past results.

- **Run with it.** The only way to test new digital strategies in a previously untested online environment is to take the risk. If you have the confidence and a good team flanking you, you will minimize the risk, take the ball, and run. Just make sure that you capture the new data so that reports can be compiled and you can address potential hiccups right away.

Think about centralizing your digital assets[24] by choosing the right reporting software and utilities for your automotive online marketing strategies. This can save you heaps of money, nerves, aggravation, time, and resources by minimizing B- and C- tasks and automating even lower priorities.

Do not forget to link your online marketing deployments with your company's overall business and offline marketing. And do not forget to own, defend, and run with your strategic vision when you know it will make a positive difference for all.

---

24   Ian Michaels, The Marketers Guide to Justifying Investments in Digital Asset Management, http://www.saepio.com/workspace/media/misc/Marketers%20 Guide%20to%20Justifying%20DAM%20Investments.pdf

DRIVING STRATEGIC OPERATIONS AND CHECKPOINT SYSTEMS

CHAPTER 5

Assembling Your Marketing Roadmap

"In preparing for battle I have always found that plans are useless, but planning is indispensable."

DWIGHT D. EISENHOWER

he moment you enter a battle zone, every soldier knows the landscape—he knows where his team members are, what they are doing, and what they need to get done in order to achieve their mission objective. To be an online marketing dealer, you will need to build or assemble a marketing roadmap for these exact reasons.

Stumbling into a new arena blind is bad enough, but when you lead a team into certain failure because you have no "Plan B" in your repertoire, that is worst of all. One of my favorite sayings is "Failing to plan is planning to fail," and this is particularly true in the world of automotive digital marketing strategy.

The 6 Ps Principle of Readiness

People who met me during conferences or meetings or worked with me in sales departments know that I am a straight talking kind of guy. I have to be known as someone who will always speak up—for my team, my employers, or others involved if that is what needs to happen. I do not hesitate to state the truth, no matter how much people do not want to hear it, and I just cannot take BS.

I keep a personal principle close to my heart, and it has worked well for me over the years. You have to have a plan or roadmap in place for your digital strategy. I call it the 6 Ps Principle of Readiness.

"Prior Planning Prevents Piss Poor Performance!"

In the daily battle of selling cars with the aid of a digital strategy, if you have no plan, you certainly will not have a strategy either. Then it is just "digital," and you might as well be paying a group of people to sit behind a computer and mess around with Pinterest or reading Yahoo news all day. It cannot and does not work.

All digital marketing strategies are made up of online assets, channels, and groups of tactics that are all governed under the title of "strategy." For each asset, there must be a strategic plan. For each online channel and each process, again, a strategic plan must be in place. Sometimes this means multiple layers of planning to build a comprehensive and executable team strategy.[25]

This Is Where All Failure Begins

Everything from web design and development, sales pages, web analytics, text message campaigns, QR codes, paid advertising,

---

25   Bernie Borges Bernie, 4 Elements of a Digital Marketing Roadmap, http://www. findandconvert.com/2012/10/4-elements-of-a-digital-marketing-roadmap/

mobile apps, ecommerce sites, outbound marketing, inbound marketing, SEO, referral or word of mouth marketing—these all need to be taken into account.

If you cannot or will not put together a roadmap for success, then you will find that your team struggles to fulfil the requirements of the digital strategy. I am certain you would not send your combat team into a battle zone blind. They would not know why they are there, what they need to get done in the allotted time, and what result they have to aim for.

The mission will fail before it has even been completed because no one has consolidated the approach and formulated the best method of getting things done. That is why a roadmap is a must—a roadmap securing the fastest, best, and most viable route to achieving a specific goal or set of objectives. Your car dealership needs to sell and service vehicles and retain and grow your customer base, but you will not succeed without having lined out the plan and having created a roadmap guiding you there.

Meticulously planned digital marketing roadmaps can drive you all the way to success. They also need constant adjustments as campaigns are run and updated along the way. If you and your tactical team realize that—during a raid—going in through a window is easier than bashing down a door, then in your next campaign, you should focus on finding more open windows.

A decent sized digital roadmap spans about 18 months[26] and works on instituting and perfecting many smaller goals along the way. This governing roadmap will tell your team what to work towards and what needs to be achieved and will help them find out how to achieve it in your specified timeframe. That is seriously powerful and much more important "motivating" stuff.

---

26   Ray Wang, Why Every Company Needs to Build a Digital Roadmap, http://www.smartt.com/insights/why-every-company-needs-build-digital-roadmap

Guesstimates, Winging It, and Other Bad Strategies

There are teams that focus on and stick to the intelligence data and data cycles received—and then there are other teams that are getting good results by simply guessing what to do. The best recipe lies in the right mixture.

According to Robert Martin, all strategies require an element of guesstimation.[27] No one can predict the future, and even the best plans can derail because of outside forces. If you waste your time trying to build a perfect strategy, you will die trying. There is no such thing as a perfect strategy! So it appears to me there must always be a Plan B in your back pocket.

Do not constantly follow the approach of just "winging it." Of course you will get some satisfactory results here and there, but if you do not have a strategy, you will not create a benchmark assisting you for future endeavors. If your brand automatically gets one thousand views on YouTube with no plan, it appears "pretty good for just winging it," but what comes next? Could I have achieved even more views if I would have supported the "winging it" factor with a bit more strategic planning, like simultaneously putting it on Vimeo, MetaCafe, etc.? Your job will be getting it to +10k, and that requires a plan.

Keep in mind that "strategic planning" can be a "boring" word in digital strategy. What I mean is that we, the Ecommerce and Online Marketing Managers have heard it so often before from our owners, presidents, and GSMs—"I don't care what you do with your online marketing as long as we sell more cars"—telling you "don't plan too long; we need some action on the showroom floor." The best you can do to overcome these obstacles is to plan thoroughly, involve your team, execute, adjust, report, and show

---

27   Robert Martin, The Big Lie of Strategic Planning, http://hbr.org/2014/01/the-big-lie-of-strategic-planning/ar/1

the results based on the planning. There will be fewer critics when you show that planning has reduced all in all advertising costs, increased phone calls, and shown more visits on Vehicle Detail Pages and more traffic on the showroom floor, also known as "Opportunities" to sell.

Treat any existing digital strategy like defusing a bomb. You know what you know, but anything could happen—and there are real consequences when you become lethargic and guess if you should clip the green or the red wire. Instead, constantly seek to learn more about your niche—in this case, digital marketing and online advertising. Visit conferences like Digital Dealer, Driving Sales Executive Summit, Internet Battle Plan, Unfair Advantage, and other groups creating others solely online marketing and Internet sales events.

Creating a Market Defense Fortress

The earlier mentioned 6 Ps principle will assist you in building a heavily fortified marketing and online sales department that will withstand sieges from competition and their online and traditional marketing activities.

"Ironclad" is the word that springs to mind. History is listing that the Korean Royal Navy in 1592 was believed to be the first to create an iron plated ship as a result of the vulnerability of wooden warships. So in order to excel at creating these digital strategy roadmaps and plans and executing them with your crack team of automotive GIs, understand that these ironclad concepts matter:

- Cover yourself from enemy fire. A plan that is based on data has merit and can be shown to your leadership teams. Justification covers you in all sorts of ways when you have taken the time to base your actions on evidence. That is what evidence-based automotive strategy is all about.

- Create bunkers for your strategic objectives. When your strategy goes wrong, your competitors may pounce. This is when it pays to have a well-thought out digital strategy in place. Protect your company's reputation, protect your team members' decisions, and have backup plans in place for damage control.

- Assume that all of your competitors online are auditing and analyzing your digital strategies. They want you to fail and will capitalize on any opportunity that you give them. If you have built a marketing fortress that is ironclad, you will not have to worry about oversights, negative comments, or competitors stealing your sales from under you.

Create and implement a defense plan.[28] When soldiers are dropped into a battle zone, they consolidate and execute until something goes wrong. Then they assume the defensive position to ward off oncoming attacks. Whether yours come from inside your company or out, it is best to have documentation and evidence of your competency.

Otherwise—and I have seen this happen—team members will lose their jobs, or you will be made to suffer terrible backlash because of your bad decisions. Defense comes first, and it starts with a great team and a solid plan. Always prepare for the worst!

Continually Improving Your Market Attack Plan

Right now you have a current plan of attack—or methods of approaching your online market using digital techniques that are working quite well. The problem with this is that once you have airlifted your team into the battle zone, there is no easy way out.

---

28   Talia Sinkinson, How to Prepare a Digital Defense Strategy – So Your Brand Gets Positive Press Even When It Comes Under Fire, http://www.bulldogreporter. com/dailydog/article/winning-pr-campaigns/how-to-prepare-a-digital-defense-strategy-so-your-brand-gets-p

If you do not continually and actively improve your market plan, you will eventually be overrun with enemy troops.[29] You will all be captured, wounded, or even worse! In other words, your digital strategy team needs to understand that on-the-job improvements to your strategy (with each campaign) are part of their job. This is what makes great teams great.

New technologies, and disruptive ones at that, are being created every day. Soon they will begin to impact your team and the way that you deliver your marketing messages to your potential customers. If you are not prepared for change—and for improvement along the way—you will fall behind and perish.

With a basic strategy that follows along a "Define – Consult – Refine – Deliver" cycle, you can use the most successful techniques from your previous campaigns and marketing strategies to ensure a certain level of reliability and stability with your team plans.

When you continually improve your market attack plan, you make sure that you are always a serious contender in the market. You want to sell cars—and lots of them—but so do your direct competitors. Aside from a strong defense plan, you need an even stronger plan of attack because they will be pursuing the same thing.

With innovation, new initiatives, new techniques and experiments, and better returns with each campaign, you will eventually discover some amazing methods of selling in your area. This is a massive competitive advantage over the other teams waiting to swoop in and steal your local traffic and sales. Get there first, and always stay a step ahead.

Do this by building your strategies around the idea that they constantly update and shed poor practices, improve on great

---

29   Nichole Kelly, Is Your Digital Strategy Designed To Fail Or designed To Deliver, http://www.socialmediaexplorer.com/social-media-marketing/is-your-digital-strategy-designed-to-fail-or-designed-to-deliver/

practices, and retrain your team to seize every market opportunity or advantage that you can along the way.

Our dealer group was challenged by a competitor dominating the truck sales in more than four states and frequently selling into our DMA as well. The marketing message of theirs clearly overstated their capabilities on what they could deliver and for what price. The consumer perceived it as "This must be true when they are saying it," but we as a group knew better. So how do you want to challenge this major player and get back the piece of your pie he has taken away? I discovered in my research that he was using a lot of assets in the old traditional marketing ways: billboards, radio, satellite and TV, and print. His online strategy was just limited on his website, seeing that his traditional marketing messages were indeed guiding the potential customers from these entities to their website or phone.

For an actually small amount of marketing dollars, I was building my Ironclad, purchasing all counties for our states and securing with this first layer of defense anyone the hostile dealer across the border, running any digital ads. The next layer of defense was now to target specific makes and models, securing those and giving me and my group exclusive ads pointing out that we were the dealer to visit. The last move was now to put a "for sale" sign into his territory, which encouraged us to also obtain his state and neighboring counties and to show "yes, we have this truck too just for a better price and more equipment."

Results: We gained back market share in less than 60 days live, received RFQs from the neighboring states via email and phone, owned our home state in truck sales, lost sold truck units decreased, and that was all for around $400 per dealership involved. I executed my strategy and hit it with full strength, just as my motto said: "Never take half-measures when doing things."

CHAPTER 6

Establishing Roadmap Checkpoints

"If the leader is filled with high ambition and if he pursues his aims with audacity and strength of will, he will reach them in spite of all obstacles."

KARL VON CLAUSEWITZ

digital strategy roadmap will tell you where you are going. But that is not all. No roadmap is complete without a start date, a completion date, and multiple checkpoints in between. Knowing how to set checkpoints for your team is critical to the ongoing digital strategy process.

Along the road to attracting more online shoppers and selling more cars, you will need strategic checkpoints.

These will enable you to:

- Assess how far you have come.
- See how much you have achieved so far during your march.
- Evaluate and adjust your strategies and path where needed.
- Estimate how much further you still have to go toward reaching your objective.

It is the only method of staying on top of the MO and achieving your goals.

The Importance of Checkpoints

In the title of this chapter, I spoke of "roadmaps"—even so, we all know that in our digital marketing landscape, these so called maps, directions, gateways, or whatever you want to call them are changing rapidly. Directions and roads someone else used yesterday that are still legit will suddenly present you with a roadblock or make you experience a detour.

I want to emphasize that you should develop an azimuth as soon as you know which objectives are set, know where you want to go with your digital strategy, establish when you need to spot check, and set off in that general direction.

These checkpoints help to re-orientate you and your team during your campaigns as you all can focus on tactical targets that need to be checked and implemented along the way.

As you launch, promote, and monitor your campaigns, you will find that adjustments need to be made, improvements noted, and new tactics gleaned from the process. When you have structured checkpoints into your strategy, it helps you stop to reassess what you are doing and redirects your resources and energy on the most pressing challenges or issues.

For example, a PPC campaign with the sole purpose of branding your dealership name is one part of your digital strategy objective. You or your SEM provider decide on a text pointing out who, where, and what your dealership name is about and hopefully implement trigger points wanting the readers and potential customers to click on this ad. Best case scenario, the PPC ad may be working out fine and hitting target numbers, but what do you do when the CTR is falling short? Answer: Establish A/B testing ads. Run them parallel for two weeks and, because of the checkpoints that you build into the process (review data and metrics on certain dates along the campaign timeline), you will be able to spot opportunities, run other tests, drop non-performing ads, and improve on results as you go.

These checkpoints therefore guarantee that you succeed with your goals and that your strategy is not just built, set, and left alone. There are too many variables in digital strategy that can affect the outcome of a campaign or long-term strategy. You will need to map out[30] your strategic journey to take advantage of real-time decision making along the way!

How to Guarantee Structural Integrity

One of the main functions of checkpoint creation is to organize a logical structure and to make this structure as sound as possible. In the military, checkpoints are safety zones where soldiers can stop, take a minute, and think about their next move. They are used in strategic operations to regroup, reassess, and reorganize priorities.

In digital strategy, this means building a marketing process map[31] or dossier. This is simply an expansive outline that details what you want to do and where you want to go from that point within a specific amount of time. In other words, it outlines what you should achieve so that you can make sure that you get there on time.

- A marketing process map literally maps out in flow-form the weeks you have to work with and the various actions that you should take, one after the other. Within each space

---

30   David Treves, Flying-by-the-seat-of-your-pants as a Digital Strategy?, http://www. australianbusiness.com.au/marketing/resources/flying-by-the-seat-of-your-pants-as-a-digital-stra

31   4 Steps to Map a Digital Strategy, http://bigthunk.com/articles/4-steps-to-map-a-digital-strategy/

of time (weeks 2–8), you will list your goals or actions accordingly.

- Each of these goals or actions are called "milestones," but they are also regularly referred to as checkpoints in the industry. Moving from milestone to milestone is a great way to assess and evaluate progress in a team environment.

An example of a few milestones might be "evaluate website X" and "evaluate current lead sources" or "price discussion with vendors on centralized purchasing power." With each milestone that you achieve, the rest may change or be altered as well.

When you begin, you may start with a 24-week period of 30 or so milestones that run along the weekly timelines. When you are finished, these milestones will be different, altered, or improved, or you may have added more in along the way.

Digital strategy needs to be organized, so structural integrity is a big one to learn. To guarantee it, always set milestones to a new strategic timeline so that improvements can be made as you go along. That is just good practice, and you will not get lost in tackling and focusing on all these multiple task to come.

How to Stay Plugged In to Your Market

A key concern for any digital dealer or strategist is the external market because it directly affects your plans, processes, and objectives. Just like a military team moving from point to point, there will be unknown threats and obstacles along the way. You cannot ignore them, and you cannot move past them, because they will negatively impact your campaigns.

This is why you have to stay plugged into your market by using adequate checkpoint markers. They help you remain aware of your external surroundings so that if anything does happen to change, your team can spring into defensive mode or attack mode depending on what has happened.

There are often new products that are launched into the market or changes in vendor relations that need to be taken into account. The last thing you need is to launch a campaign expecting one thing to go through with, and then, for example, your website vendor recants on services they provided but were essential in your thought process on being able to implement a successful strategy. It happened to me, and I can guarantee it will lead to a lot of unhappy conversations and discussion (or should I say yelling matches) between you and your vendor.

Being aware of your surroundings begins with checkpoint analysis. At each milestone, your team will pause, check that everything is still 100% on track, and then head out to the next checkpoint. If this does not happen, any number of issues can arise along the way that will worsen with every checkpoint that you ignore or do not have.

Plug yourself into your external market by considering the positive impact checkpoints can have on any digital roadmap— short or long term. My advice would be to take a course in strategic roadmapping[32] or to at least invest in some strategic roadmapping software.

If you have not done tertiary education in marketing structures, then you may need some help putting together your initial maps and milestones. Attempting to put together an entire digital strategy without them is going to be time consuming and fairly disastrous.

Even if you are able to manage the many tasks required, you will not have the checkpoints in place to keep your strategy on target, and it will derail. Somewhere along the way, your metrics will plummet, and you will lose conversions and sales.

---

32   Mapping Marketing Processes for Automation – Save Time and Increase Efficiency, http://www.pardot.com/webinars/recorded-webinar-mapping-marketing-processes-automation/

Consistency Using Checkpoints

Checkpoints are beneficial because they make room for continued consistency in your digital strategy frameworks and roadmaps. Consistency is one of the most important elements of any digital strategy because it keeps you up to date on your company culture and any changes that may impact the marketing messages you are sending out into the world.

What your brand or company says to the world matters, which is why the ability to communicate an effective and consistent online image is paramount to good digital strategy. While there will always be team members with their own ideologies, ideas, and values, these should never impact your decisions.

The only way to prevent outside opinions from taking hold is to have a clear idea of what your company culture is and how you have chosen to communicate that through integrated media and consistent digital strategy.

With high levels of consistency comes instant brand recognition and cross channel flow, and your target consumers will be more comfortable trusting your various online touch points because they come from you. Everything from message longevity[33] to the verbiage that you use can change over time, and you need to be on top of this.

All online marketing oriented dealers that want to keep their team fully aligned with their brand image, company culture, and policies should take checkpoint analysis very seriously. This is where inconsistencies are picked up and sorted out before any damage can be done.

Think of it as a way of ensuring that if your team did do something wrong between the last checkpoint and your new one,

---

33   Monique Merhige, Consistency Is Key in Your Integrated Marketing Strategy, http://digitalethos.org/consistency-is-key-in-your-integrated-marketing-strategy/

you can make certain it never happens again by analyzing what transpired between specific time periods. Be the leader that keeps things constant!

The Follow-Up Checkpoint Guide

When your online strategy roadmap has no checkpoints to speak of, there will be absolutely zero follow-up process. In digital marketing, one of the most successful methods of converting leads into sales is the humble and consistent follow up. It can be used in a multitude of contexts and across many different and important media or platform touch points.

A follow-up process map is what you create to support your running marketing process dossier. Everything from your automated leads to manual follow-up processes must be outlined here, along a daily timeline. Using simple color coordination, you can put together a practical follow-up dossier outlining when and what you need to do during your campaigns.

A few examples might be to phone certain clients, to send return emails, or to conduct management surveys. When you do not have these clearly outlined follow-up checkpoints, you will lose an abundance of potential leads and clients along the way.

Marketing processes might get you that lead, but it still needs to be converted. Creating a following up process map will tell your team what they need to get done to drive home the lead and sell more cars, more often! If you do not bother with follow ups, then I would say just find another job other than the car sales profession.

Memory is not going to work for so many different campaigns and marketing entities. If you do not document your strategy correctly, it will not be managed correctly—which is your job as an ecommerce person.

TIP: Look around in the lunch or meeting room of your dealership and see if you have a huge wall space available. Then print out all communications you have lined up in your process and pin them in "what happens on Day X and following" order. It will assist your team members and new joining fellows to learn and memorize what is expected from them down the path. It will also show transparency to the rest of the dealership sales force and management, showing that you are in control of the things you have planned out, and underlines your yang and determination for success for the entire dealership.

"Sorry for not getting back to you" should become a phrase that you never use.[34] Make it your business to transform your team, and hopefully the entire dealership, into follow-up pros.

Accountability With Checkpoint Achievement

The final reason why checkpoints and milestones are a necessary part of your digital strategy roadmap is that they promote accountability. With every checkpoint that you reach, there will be a review process that needs to be conducted.

Think about a band of brothers during a mission. They made it to their next checkpoint. What do they do? Next to possibly having a quick bite and refueling with some protein bars, they check their gear to see if everything is still working and in existence. The same should be done by you and your team when you will pause. Check that everything is still aligned and on track, and if something has gone wrong, you will easily be able to find out why and what happened right then and there. It is about the *now* and not later.

Try determining what went wrong four months after a campaign was run. It just will not happen. When you use milestones, everyone is accountable because it becomes a process of short-term analysis.

---

34   Why You Need a Follow Up Sales Strategy, http://tresnicmedia.com/why-you-need-a-follow-up-sales-strategy/

When you can look back over a short timeframe, details and intricacies that would have been lost can be spotted and acted upon. With no checkpoints, there is no accountability! As I mentioned earlier, the one thing that plagues dedicated online dealers in our field is that too often shown a total lack of accountability. Budgets are no laughing matter, and neither is a team run amok.

REMINDER

- Checkpoints will help you effectively manage your budgets. You will not overspend, and any excess can be reassigned where it will make the most impact.

- Checkpoints will help you keep your measurement processes on track due to the fact that analytics has a way of changing constantly.

- Checkpoints help your team to stop and look at the entire campaign from an "overall" point of view to spot obvious issues. Alignment and objective achievement is everything.

- Checkpoints will make sure that if you have been doing something incorrectly, sloppy, or in the wrong manner, you can immediately stop it, improve it, or replace it early.

With this kind of strategic communication planning,[35] your entire team will remain accountable for everything that they do. All decisions, actions, and results will be easily traceable to specific people at specific times. No one will be able to remain silent if they have genuinely done something to cause negative backlash during your campaigns.

Now you know why one of my favorite German proverbs is "Trust is good—control is better."

---

[35] Dawn Hepper, The Accountability Project: A 10 Step Plan to Reach Your Digital Marketing Goals, http://www.ciceron.com/2014/03/accountability-project-10-step-plan-reach-digital-marketing-goals/

section 4

DRIVING IN ENEMY TERRITORY USING IN-HOUSE TACTICAL RESPONSES

CHAPTER 7

Understanding Your Ferocious Market Enemy

"And while the law of competition may be sometimes hard for the individual, it is best for the race, because it ensures the survival of the fittest in every department."

ANDREW CARNEGIE

n Section 4, I will take you through the realities of competitive car sales online, along with how your in-house team can become exceptionally good at staying a step ahead of your competitors so that you can close more sales than ever before.

It is vitally important to understand that the moment you begin to market online, you are in enemy territory. Your competitors can and will hijack your practices, and some of them may even use black hat techniques to steal traffic from your sites.

What Your Enemy Knows About You

The tougher the competition, the healthier the online automotive industry becomes. This is because nearly everything can be reverse engineered online thanks to a little thing called data.

When you approach online marketing—while keeping your competitors in mind—you can improve your processes, practices, and content more efficiently. The truth is that your competitors have a lot more to do with your online sales approach than you think.

Understanding your competitive landscape is key to securing your place there. Other online dealers have their eye on you. They have most likely already audited your websites, painstakingly mapped out your social campaigns, reviewed your reputation handled online, and analyzed your SEO as well SEM on a micro level. Everything they need, they can find to get a one up on your team.

Your competition certainly looked at a recent survey report by JD Power and Associates,[36] which suggests that 64% of 18- to 24-year-old consumers want their car dealerships to respond to them when they mention the brand online. So they did not necessary send an inbound email or place a phone call but more likely talked about you and your dealership somewhere out there in the world wide web. Monitoring this content means getting there first, before your competition does.

With multiple competitors knowing everything there is to know about your strategies, you need to ask yourself right away, "How much do I really know about them?" Perhaps it is time to find out.

Tapping the Wires on Your Competition

The Internet is not an abstract place. It is a real place, with real geographical locations and limitations. Areas and properties can be seized just like they can be on any street corner in America.

---

36   Ralph Paglia, Car Dealers Must Monitor The Social Web To Remain Competitive, http://www.dealermarketing.com/internet-marketing/social-media/3037-car-dealers-must-monitor-the-social-web-to-remain-competitive

The last thing you want is for all of your potential customers to be buying on the other side of the street! I remember my early-on times handling the Internet leads in our little town, and then, when sitting at the red light, noticing that the new car with the license plate frame mounted was not from our franchise. I just hated it.

That is why you need to start ASAP by recording, analyzing, and integrating all business and competitive intelligence from your top competitors. The guys across the street or town that you know are bugging you the most and harming your dealership's bottom line.

- Know what your local, national, and international markets are doing in a context that will help your team sell better and build larger communities for repeat sales. That means finding out what they are doing on social, reputation, service offers, etc.

- Knowledge is power, and you should conduct a complete online brand presence audit of your top 10 competitors. Know what they are selling and how they are selling it, and review what their overall marketing goals are for their various online properties, like Autotrader, Cars.com, and KKB, to name just a few.

- Perform a SWOT analysis on your competition. Focus on uncovering exactly who they are and what their intentions are online. Stay up to date to keep your team well-informed. The last thing you want is for your tactical team to wander into a minefield. There are many social minefields out there that can be blundered into, so monitoring in real-time is a must.

Try to see everyone in your car dealership as a potential intelligence resource. Armed Forces has a saying that "every soldier is a sensor," so use this to your advantage.[37] Get each team member involved in the consistent analysis of your competition to stay streets ahead of them at all times. Competitive knowledge extends far beyond what you can find out online.

Remember that the goal with competitive intelligence is to gather information on your enemies that your team can *act* on. This actionable information will help you side step minefields, sneak by enemy troops, and ultimately claim the landscape as your own.

The Lay of the Land: Business Intelligence Orientation

To get an accurate "lay of the land," as they say, you will need to perform a basic SWOT analysis on each of your competitors. Your online sales team may not have much experience in this regard, so you will need to lead the charge here.

The very survival of your job and success of your digital strategies relies on your ability to effectively conduct these SWOT analyses.[38] Once you have conducted your analysis, you will be better positioned to retaliate, attack, or defend with your next campaign.

- *Strengths* – These make your competitors better than you, so it is a good idea to know what they are. They can include anything from a great brand identity, to strong content assets, to a formidable track record with digital strategy.

- *Weaknesses* – These make your competitors vulnerable and can show you areas that you could exploit for your own benefit. Where is their performance lacking? Where could

---

37   Burt Helm, How to Use Competitive Intelligence to Gain an Advantage, http://www.inc.com/magazine/20110401/how-to-use-competitive-intelligence-to-gain-an-advantage.html

38   SWOT Analysis – A Key Competitive Intelligence Tool, http://ci4winstrategy.com/uploads/SWOTAnalysis.pdf

they use a lot of additional time, resources, or strategy? Where could you simply and easily outdo them?

- *Opportunities* – With an eye on your competition, you will be able to judge them based on what is happening in your DMA. Identify trends, demand for certain cars, or new market segments just by watching your immediate competition.

- *Threats* – Market trends can go south, and they often do with big assets like cars. Watch for competitors running ridiculous sales prices that steal your business or new regulations impacting your market. All potential threats must be monitored so that you can catch them as they happen.

Business intelligence orientation is about knowing your place in the market by understanding what your competitors are doing. Imagine a tactical military squad unleashed in a new arena with no information on their enemies—they would be completely blind to all external eventualities whether positive or negative.

Make sure that you continually audit your competition, like mystery shopping, service flexibilities, or telephone responses, so that you can see threats coming while taking advantage of all positive opportunities for your brand or dealership. That is what will make you and your team formidable digital warriors.

Behind the Scenes: Gaining the Upper Hand

There are many marketing processes that go on behind the scenes that will contribute to a thorough competitive analysis of your digital marketing competition. It is important to remember that your team needs to be positioned to gain the upper hand at all times when it comes to competitor relations.

That is why the practice of mystery shopping can be so revealing. Defined, mystery shopping is when a team member or third party undergoes your competitor's customer experience so that they can fully understand how it works.

This includes an online customer experience audit along with real world visits and engagement with competitor staff and processes. Mystery shopping is also a quality control measure for marketers that want to make sure their marketing teams are firing on all cylinders.

For your tactical team, this is literally about venturing behind enemy lines. An undercover agent will pose as a customer and will be walked through all of your enemy's practices in real time. They hopefully will mentally and physically record the experience to streamline your SWOT analysis and make it more realistic. Otherwise, how will you know where the weak spots are to attack?

You can bet that your competition has already sent over some covert teams to do some mystery shopping of their own. Or at least they send email requests for a proposal to see how fast you are responding, what you are saying in your response, whether you are giving a price via responses, what the price structures you use are, and so on and so on. They have spotted your strengths and have seen the opportunities that you have left them. It is a constant battlefield of will—where the team that does the best work wins. The "best" can be defined as the most consistent and the most strategic.

When your team combines all insight for your dealership, they will have enough information on the key players in your local market to probably launch a full blown plan of attack. If you are smart, it will target an area that your enemies have not capitalized on yet.

Transform your team into highly competitive online sales and marketing troops[39] by educating them on the merits of "knowing

---

39   Jim Larranaga, Mystery Shopping Gains Momentum in the Digital Age, http://www.bluespiremarketing.com/blog/March-2013/mystery-shopping-gains-momentum-in-the-digital-age

your enemy." Another tip: You should definitely send mystery shoppers to your own branches as well so that you can see and hear exactly what your customers are experiencing when they write, call, or drop by for a potential purchase.

Approach With Caution: Direct or Stealth Strategy?

In the realm of digital strategy, you will need to assess your competitors correctly and then make educated decisions about how to approach your local or even regional market.

There are four main methods of approaching a new campaign or strategy, and it depends on the kind of team that you have assembled and what your competitors are doing.

The first method I call "attack your competition head on." This kind of marketing warfare has been around for a long time, and it can definitely become more impactful since the Internet has begun to serve as an accelerant of news and brand messages.

One of the most known and talked about automotive marketing "attacks straight on" is the Audi and BMW dispute in California. Audi placed a huge "New Audi A4" billboard ad near Santa Monica Blvd. The message: "Chess? No thanks, I'd rather be driving. - The entirely new Audi A4." Well, so far nothing really unusual and pretty much unaggressive. When Audi replaced this ad in April, it suddenly read a little bit more snarky and targeted the direct competition, BMW, with the phrase "Your move, BMW." Boom—this strike was definitely delivered.

Sure enough, BMW acquired a larger billboard just across from Audi's signage and showed their A4 competitor model—a BMW M3 partnered with just one word: "Checkmate." Nice comeback, but whoever thought that Audi would have been waving the white flag of surrender did not see the next move coming at all.

Even so, the turf war started and was handled in old-fashioned, a.k.a. offline advertising, here: Using a billboard in a small section of a city with more than 16 million in their area, Audi utilized its masses and the fans they had added on their social media marketing channels over time.

With asking their Facebook followers to post their responses to BMW's latest attack in the form of a Photoshopped picture right next to the M3 billboard, they suddenly had a mighty force, and even better, the fight had gone viral. Maximum exposure in all online channels!

Result: The BMW ad disappeared, and Audi put one more finger into the open wound of their public enemy. Another ad was developed, this time with an Audi R8 stating, "Time to check your luxury badge. It may have expired."

By employing online, offline, and social marketing strategies simultaneously, you will have great chances to secure your competitive advantage.

With direct attacks, you want your customers to know that you have bettered your competition. The purpose of these marketing attacks is to hang a negative on a competitor so that you can enhance a positive from your brand.[40]

The second method is to attack by stealth. This is done by taking advantage of an opportunity that you have discovered from one of your competitors. Instead of attacking them directly, you will simply seize market share by outbidding them on their keyword-specific ads and by knocking them off the top spot on Google.

This can be done using digital content campaigns, brilliant SEO campaigns, and a number of other converged media options. When your brand or dealership is being spoken about the most, people forget about your competitors. A stealth attack is the exact

---

40   Jack Trout, Brand Strategy: Set Up a Positive and Attack, http://www. brandingstrategyinsider.com/2012/05/brand-strategy-set-up-a-positive-and-attack. html#.U8PX5PmSySo

reason why you need to monitor your competitors, especially the local ones.

Market Maneuvering: Surround or Out Flank?

In the military—and now with digital strategy—the other two methods of staying ahead of your competitors involve surrounding or out flanking them on the digital battlefield.[41] This is commonly known as out maneuvering your competition, and it often involves being much more innovative and taking larger risks than they are prepared to take.

As a guerrilla marketing tactic, surrounding your competitor involves pre-emptive strikes, frontal attacks, making strategic alliances, and deterring your competition from directly attacking you by sheer show of strategic ability and digital wizardry.

- Surround your competitors online by being better than them on all fronts. Have an innovative, responsive website design ensuring a perfect display of your virtual stores on all entities, such as iPad, mobile phone, desktop, etc. According to Marketing Blog,[42] 67 percent of website visitors would be more likely to purchase from mobile-friendly websites. Have the best and engaging social media channels, such as Facebook, Twitter, Pinterest, Google+, and focus on creating outstanding YouTube videos for your brand. All of these are methods of surrounding and eventually snuffing out your competitors.

In the real world, this is akin to a customer searching a term online and discovering your competitor at the top of page 1 of Google. However, you have all of the ad space and the next five

---

41   Allan, Elder, Five Targets of Competitive Attack On Your Business, http://biznik.com/articles/five-targets-of-competitive-attack-on-your-business

42   http://www.marketingtechblog.com/2014-digital-marketing-roadmap/

spots on Google. You have effectively encircled your competitor and made them look insignificant by sheer show of presence.

- Flanking your competitors in the digital arena is all about focusing on niche areas that are of little importance to your direct competitors. They do not even bother in these segments, which means that they are wide open to you. Strengthen the way you flank your competition by exploring new ways to sell or service new markets and better methods of selling on a consistent basis.

Online, your team may discover that directly attacking a huge dealership brand is not going to get them anywhere, because they are outmatched. On further investigation, you may discover that your competitor does not bother marketing to baby boomers any more, for example. If this is the case, you can launch a wildly successful campaign with little resistance at all.

Use these excellent battle-tested strategic techniques to outmaneuver your competition. These competitors will take your customers and launch direct attacks on your local market, so be prepared for them. Think ahead, and find methods of defeating these enemies!

CHAPTER 8

Enemy Approach and Weapon Selection

"Number one, cash is king...number two, communicate...number three, buy or bury the competition."

ANDREW CARNEGIE

It is fair to say that in the automotive online marketing arena, direct competition is fierce. It is your team versus whoever else wants to stake a claim on your sales and services, however expansive they may be. I have suggested some basic methods of approaching your competition. It does not really matter who has the best website. (Who actually determines what is best?) It only matters who receives the most opportunities to have customers show up at your brick and mortar locations and convert them into the most car sales or happy and returning service customers.

Guerrilla marketing[43] is an aggressive form of marketing offensive that utilizes the power of unusual, unexpected, or shock-

---

43   Ashley Manker, What Is Guerilla Marketing? – Definition, Strategies & Examples, http://education-portal.com/academy/lesson/what-is-guerrilla-marketing-definition-strategies-examples.html#lesson

tactic marketing to attract as much attention from as many people as possible. Strategies can include honoring your competitor's coupons, price matches, or beating their deal specials.

The Four A's of Overcoming the Enemy

Once you have made your decision about your method of approach— or perhaps your strategy will include multiple campaigns using different forms of approach (depending on your team size)—you will need to understand how to overcome your enemy.

In the military, there are some plans that work over and over again in different situations. These strategic models[44] can be perfected by your team over time. I like to call mine the four A's of overcoming the enemy's surge.

The four A's are: Approach, Answer, Alternative, and Activate.

- Begin by *approaching* your market customers with fresh, new ideas. Do not be afraid to try out new things, as all buying segments are different. Ideas are the creative forces that help you sell more cars with digital strategy. Invite your team to become a part and possible experts in brainstorming and idea generation for your dealership.

- The next step is to *answer* your customers by tending to their questions and making sure that all inquiries are handled flawlessly. Communication sells cars, and yours need to be modern, engaging, and incredibly effective. Think about personalized video answers and video walkarounds as an answer to common customer questions.

- Consider playing around with *alternative* pricing models when giving price quotes on your cars. Your pricing models

---

44   Justin Fried, How to Decipher Your Competitors Digital Marketing Strategy, http://searchenginewatch.com/article/2181586/How-to-Decipher-Your-Competitors-Digital-Marketing-Strategy

and matrixes close the deal. At the end of the day, most car sales come down to pitch and price. Be flexible, be innovative, and allow for outside-the-box pricing to win over your customer's loyalty. Club member discounts and charity selections are two methods of doing this.

- The last step is to *activate*. A top-notch VIP experience is what your customers deserve when buying a vehicle. It matters what happens in-house, or your online conversions will plunge. Make the "real life" experience twice as good as what the customer expects, and close those sales.

When approaching a new market—or an existing one—it is imperative to keep the four A's in mind so that you have a viable process to work through. New ideas, supporting and communicating with your customers, preparing your pricing models, and treating your customers like VIPs when they hit the showroom will result in more sales and more retention for all profit centers.

Choose Your Weapon!

When you and your team have decided on your approach to the market—and to keep your enemies at bay—you will need to select your weaponry. In the military, a team is only as good as its assembly, and teams are usually handpicked for specializations according to the mission at hand.

This can be a handy piece of insight when selecting your own weapons for your upcoming digital strategy battle. With multiple opponents—and many that you may not even be aware of—weapon selection is more important than ever. Focus on the strength of the weapons that you choose to make your strategies stronger and more effective.

- Customer relationship management is a key weapon of choice in the ongoing battle for more car sales. The way that you communicate, respond to, and support your customer's needs will inevitably determine how well your messages work.

- Your campaigns need to be powerful weapons against your competitors, either outdoing them in certain ways or taking advantage of areas that they have not targeted yet. Your competitors are out there, and they are watching you. Your campaigns are the sword that will keep them at bay.

- Branding is another great weapon in your fight against the enemy—and your branding on and offline needs to be consistent, highly recognizable, and unique among everyone else in your competitor pool. Stand out by being different and by delivering that difference with strong, clear-branded messages.

If you can use competent CRM[45] and strong branding with a powerful campaign, competitors will have trouble touching you. Then it is just a matter of tweaking the details in your favor to make those sales objectives. Digital strategy is not about copying your competitors; it is about understanding their motives, knowing yours, and doing something original.

With my many years of experience, I am still satisfied with an original idea that contains these vital elements or sales weapons. You can make most strategies work if you run campaigns that focus closely on these. It is unlikely that your competition will be able to damage you if your team has taken the steps necessary to defend their approaches.

---

45   Lars Crama, Bridging the Gap Between CRM and Digital Marketing – In 5 Steps, http://www.slideshare.net/larscrama/bridging-the-gap-between-crm-and-digital-marketing

Focus That Weapon Reach

To challenge the status quo and seize back some of your lost market share, you need to focus your weapon reach by consolidating and building viable campaigns or strategies that focus exclusively on visibility or reach.

The more people that see your brand and your messages, the more they are likely to listen to what you have to say. Who you reach, when, and how matters in digital strategy because it will determine how they engage, think about, recall, and share your marketing messages.

- Your dealership reputation is still an understated weapon that must be used. Automotive reputation management is not easy, but it counts. According to Cobalt,[46] there is a serious lack of reviews on car dealership websites, and many reviews only reflect a 2.1 star rating, a far cry from the 3.5 star glass ceiling.

- That same study conducted by Cobalt across 2,500 dealerships concluded that reviews were instrumental to dealership sales. Stars impact car sales! Even Harvard supported this research stating that the more stars a site has, the more traffic and revenue it generates. Arm yourself with quality reviews—lots of them.

- Advertising in this instance can be an epic weapon to harness reach for your automotive brand. According to a research study,[47] online video advertising is 200% more effective than television advertising, for example.

---

46   The Street Smart Guide to Automotive Reputation Management Ebook, http://www.cobalt.com/industry-insights/the-street-smart-guide-to-reputation-management/

47   Ralph Paglia, Research Study Shows Online Video Advertising Is 200 Percent More Effective Than TV, http://www.automotivedigitalmarketing.com/profiles/blogs/research-study-shows-online-video-advertising-is-200-percent-more

If the goal is to get your brand messages seen by the right people, you have to be where your target audience hangs out. Focus on media that they enjoy and embrace. Direct your ad reach by keeping it in line with your sales goals and weapon choices.

Formulating Strategic Approach Combos

Nothing in digital marketing stands alone, and you will find that the best strategies are made up of a combination of strategic approach combos so that you can knock out your competition. The right combination will always get the job done, and that is the crux of your role as your dealership's online marketer.

It is up to you to pick the right approaches and weaponry so that you can invade enemy territory and seize some of the market for yourself. This means pairing online and offline approaches to create converged, integrated media strategies that exceed anything your customers have seen thus far.

Build a brand strategy that gets rid of the old traditional marketing siloes that have made it so hard for teams like yours to function in this field! I am speaking about governing all of your marketing activities under one clear brand strategy and uniting your marketing approaches under one single goal.

You cannot fit a 45 cal clip into a Glock 9mm gun. In the same way, you cannot expect to sell cars online like old traditional marketing teams once did. More goes into it now, and it matters how adapted your brand feels, looks, and behaves in all online marketing channels.

By pinpointing the right approach for each campaign and gathering your correct weapons, you will be fully armed with a logical plan of action at the ready. In the military, no team can move without these two elements. Only one additional element remains, and that is the vehicle that you will use to get there.

Picking the right weapon at the right time is a critical skill that you need to train into your team. Focus on short-term, mid-range, and long-range results using these initial two methods of structuring your automotive digital strategy. Use paid, owned, and earned media![48]

An example of a strategic attack combo might be a dealership hosting an event, using paid hashtags to promote that event via Twitter, writing a series of blog posts that contain guest showcases, and creating a set of three YouTube-centric videos that upsell your car products based on researched keywords that will click with the audience. This, tied to a comprehensive PPC campaign and adding Facebook's mobile ads, will get you the results that you need.

---

48   Tara DeMarco, The First 6 Steps to Successful Converged Media (Paid, Owned, and Earned), http://blog.bazaarvoice.com/2012/10/03/the-first-6-steps-to-successful-converged-media-paid-owned-and-earned/

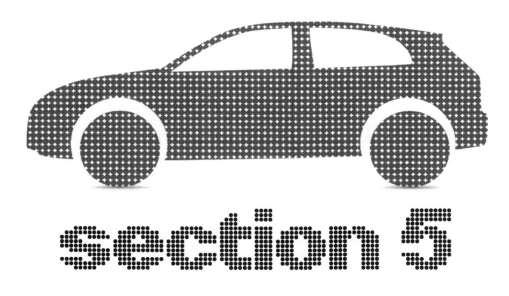

section 5

DRIVING POSITIVE CHANGE WITH THE RIGHT VEHICLE SELECTION

CHAPTER 9

The Science of Vehicle Marketing

"Marketing is telling the world you're a rock star. Content Marketing is showing the world you are one."

ROBERT ROSE

Digital automotive strategy relies heavily on the vehicles that you choose to use for each campaign or within your ongoing strategies. By now, you should have chosen your preferred approach and the weapons that you are going to use.

All that remains is to familiarize yourself with the many vehicle choices that you have. These vehicles will help you attain that much desired reach and those sales conversions that your dealership desperately needs. It is up to you; here is the science behind it.

How to Build Your Fleet Using the Right "Vehicles"

Assembling a force for war is a daunting task for any online marketer, and that is exactly what you face—a full blown war. There will be many battles—internal as well as external—and your sales will reflect who is winning them. The great thing about the Internet is that you cannot hide from the results.

That is why you need to know how to decide on the right vehicle to use. You will do this by conducting business and market intelligence. Some 18.2 sources of influence online will more likely dictate the decision that your shopper will make along the way. Seven of the top eight influences are from the discovery phase when purchasing a car online.

An easier way of putting it is that sales result mainly from direct search engine searches, dealership inventory searches, and searches on manufacturer's websites. After that, it comes down to personal recommendations, reviews, and referrals. You have control over all of these elements along the discovery phase because you can control your own online brand presence.

Vehicles for getting your information and marketing messages out include your primary owned websites, general digital advertising, online and offline marketing, online classifieds, and using the social media approach. Using combinations of these, you can effectively guide potential leads to visit you versus the competition.

Air Vehicles: SEO, Native Advertising, Aggregators, Retargeting

I have split up the most important vehicles into air, land, and water vehicles. Any good military force that is moving into battle needs to approach the battlefield from multiple directions using multiple tactics. These vehicles—and the campaigns within them—will help you achieve the ultimate goal of reaching more consumers.

Air vehicles for your armed forces include SEO, native advertising, aggregators, and retargeting. These air vehicles seem to work behind the scenes, but they are an incredibly important part of your brand reputation and presence online.

- **SEO:** Search engine optimization[49] techniques make up the wings that will fly your campaigns and messages to new heights. Understand how modern search engines generate results, and streamline all of your unique content and practices to meet these requirements for more reach, conversions, and sales.

- **Native advertising:** This air vehicle involves using paid advertising techniques in an informational way, as it is done in content marketing. According to IPG Media Lab,[50] native ads are viewed the same number of times as editorial content, but they are much more likely to be shared than banner ads. Examples are promoted tweets, sponsored Facebook posts, and banner ads in YouTube videos.

- **Aggregators:** This particular air vehicle[51] helps you reach beyond your own or OEM-owned websites. Internet sales lead aggregators like LotLinx, Dealix, Autobytel, and others can capture a lot of business for you and help bring more people to your websites.

- **Retargeting:** The final air vehicle for your aerial digital strategy assault involves bringing back your visitors by keeping track of who visits your website and displaying reminder ads to them as they visit other third party sites online. This helps your message reach the right people at the right time and on the right platform.

---

49   Search Engine Optimization, http://www.gforces.co.uk/total-digital-marketing/view/364/seo

50   Infographic: Native Advertising Effectiveness Study by IPG Media Lab and Sharethrough, http://www.sharethrough.com/2013/05/infographic-native-advertising-effectiveness-study-by-ipg-media-labs/

51   Dean Evans, Internet Lead Aggregators: Be Everywhere on the Web for $200 Per Vehicle, http://www.dealermarketing.com/internet-marketing/online-marketing/472-internet-lead-aggregators-be-everywhere-on-the-web-for-200-per-vehicle

With SEO and these excellent modern advertising techniques, you can make sure that your car buyers can always find you if they search for you or that they return to your dealership or brand if they happen to be on social platforms or third party networks. Catching your leads at the right time is important, and this rapidly improves your chances.

Land Vehicles: OEM Alignment and Online/ Offline Coordination

Down on the ground, your special ops team will need to make sure that your land vehicles are working for your benefit. Of all the various vehicles, these are the ones that cause the most conversions and result in the most sales. Think of them as the rolling tanks, artillery, and ground units that you need to win the war. They always need to be prepared.

The OEM Marketing message alignment is important for your dealership. National OEM aligned websites and their digital advertising campaigns exist to help you tell your potential online customers, "Yes, I am also participating in the 'sign then drive event,'" or similar.

Make sure that your OEM goals are aligned with your own. You will also want to look into online and offline coordination of your various media properties. They need to be aligned and in sync so that you can boast about a consistent brand strategy that works.

Things like special Landing Pages, SEM and SEO revamps and updates, owner marketing, mobile marketing, and event marketing are all part of this segment.

The truth is that digital strategies are now dominating the purchasing journey for most people.[52]

---

52   Jan-Christoph Kostring, Eight Trends Shaping Digital Marketing in the Auto Industry, http://www.mckinsey.com/client_service/marketing_and_sales/latest_thinking/eight_trends_shaping_digital_marketing_in_the_auto_industry

Everything from networking, in-house collaboration, customer rewards and referrals, business partnerships, and marketing materials must all be aligned and integrated into your new method of working with automotive digital strategy. If your online presence does not reflect your offline presence—or vice versa—you will lose momentum, and you will appear disconnected.

Water Vehicles: Websites, Landing Pages, Event Pages, SEM

The final group of vehicles to consider are the properties themselves. These owned and earned webpages will keep your sales afloat as they make up the bulk of your online presence. Different vehicles travel at different speeds.

Your Facebook page may take six months to convince a buyer to check you out locally and give the service department a try. They all work differently, but they all need to be consistent, recognizable, and populated with engaging and unique content. Sites like these that do not have great content will sink into the depths of the cyber ocean, especially considering that Google and Co. as well as their constant changes in algorithm make it harder for websites to rank high in the SERPs.

Your websites and its webpages must be focused on consumer engagement, interesting and unique information, and conversion, along with your microsites and various landing pages online. The same goes for any isolated event pages or websites that you launch for special contests or promotions. Search engine marketing needs to be performed for all of these to keep traffic hitting them.

Consider active reputation management by being present and consistently engaging with potential leads on all your sites. Everything from blogging, live chats, and engaging on social media matters because it makes up part of your overall CRM strategy. You could have the nicest and most modern dealership building in the world, but if consumers are not helped when they need it—or engaged with when they want to engage—you may lose them totally.

A just released survey data[53] from Lithium Technologies seems to underline the above mentioned theory. The data showed that 70% of Twitter users expected a response from brands they had reached out to on Twitter. Fifty-three percent of those users wanted this to happen in less than an hour!

Even more disturbing in this conducted survey is that there are harsh consequences for a poor response performance, which showed almost 30% will tell friends and family about the bad experience. Every fourth person will consider buying less from that company, and 15% will shame this performance via other social media channels! Can I get a B O O M?!?!

Your water vehicles will convert a flood of traffic for you, and it is where all of your other marketing tactics should point. All ads should lead to owned media sites, and all promotions must be supported by information—which is best delivered in content form, whether that content is text, conversation, images, audio, or video.

From your primary website presence, your page's landing pages, and your OEM sites to collaborative online and offline marketing entities to enhance your digital strategy to getting results from online classifieds and third party sites, to approaching the social Internet with great content and brilliant conversation—all content needs to be mapped out, planned, and built before your digital strategy will be successful.

To recap: Select your approach, identify your weapons, choose your vehicles, and begin formulating one heck of a good digital campaign for your brand or dealership.[54]

---

53   Pamela Vaughan. 72% of People Who Complain on Twitter Expect a Response Within an Hour. http://blog.hubspot.com/marketing/twitter-response-time-data

54   David Pritchard, The Three Phases of Dealership Digital Marketing, http://www.autodealermonthly.com/channel/dps-office/article/story/2011/08/the-three-phases-of-dealership-digital-marketing.aspx

CHAPTER 10

Focus on Strategy and Avoid Rushing

"Rushing into action, you fail. Trying to grasp things, you lose them. Forcing a project to completion, you ruin what was almost ripe..."

LAO TZU, TAO TE CHING

The biggest threat to an automotive digital strategy—and to the success of your team—is rush. You have to avoid rushing and skipping essential steps in the process. Get your team to focus on the process and finding the right strategy to use to launch and run smart online campaigns using multiple vehicles.

There is serious power in focus. From what I have learned and observed, a majority of dealerships fail at their digital strategy because they are not willing to put in the groundwork in building a foundation and most likely skipping too fast through each step.

Overcoming Obstacles and Harnessing Focus

In a digital marketing strategy, you will realize that the more campaigns you run, the more obstacles you come into contact with. Welcome these roadblocks and barriers because it will give your team the opportunity to learn and to figure out how to overcome these obstacles that block your path to success. Learning by doing is essential, and I keep it like Sir Richard Branson, who said, "If somebody offers you an amazing opportunity but you are not sure you can do it, say yes—then learn how to do it later!"

Whether you are dealing with obstacles that are preventing your customers from trusting you[55] or something more tangible like SEO concerns, each issue is an opportunity for you to find a better solution to improve your plan of attack and to grow. Every time you run a campaign your, team should level up, prepare for some rough patches down the road, and improve in experience as they go. Keep in mind that obstacles are not the mission objective but the end results.

See your target, and hit that target. This is your primary objective. The key to this is to focus on the MO as it is one of the most important revenue-producing activities that exist. Establish goals for every mission—and if you do not achieve them within your timeline, find out why! Digital strategy is as much about solution application as it is about content.

When an obstacle arises, step back, re-evaluate the situation, and adjust your strategy. Then do it all over again until you hit your target.

Tunnel-Vision: Sniping the Target

Working during the last nine years in the field of dealerships' online strategies was not always a walk in the park. We can certainly say here that there is always something going on, and we would sometimes like to have 25 hours in a day. There are

---

55   Mike Gorun, Identify & Remove the Obstacles to Customer Loyalty, http://
www.automotivedigitalmarketing.com/profiles/blogs/identify-remove-the-obstacles-to-
customer-loyalty

dozens of things on a daily basis that can and certainly will distract you and your team from your objectives. As you become more comfortable and seasoned due to these tasks, you will also determine to one point that you cannot let that happen any longer.

Let's quickly take a look at how a sniper team is operating. Their MO is taking out the target. Next to finding a concealed position, deploying the right weapon, and having a great spotter as partner, they also need to take into account hiding the muzzle flash and masking the sound, wind, sun, and even heat. To make sure no other distraction will occur, the shooter will just focus on the target through a scope that is much narrower than the scope that his partner, the spotter, is using. We are speaking here of "being in the zone" or creating the "tunnel vision" and funneling all attention just to the main objective—the target! The spotter will tell the shooter where the target is, what the distance will be, and what the wind's speed and blowing direction is, and the shooter follows only these directions. Talk about a routine of a process that will be done over and over again—and is successful.

That is why I suggest implementing processes that help you and your team adopt a "tunnel vision" approach to your online strategy goals. When you have done all you can—and you are out there on the field of battle—you must focus only on your conversions. Set your mission goals, be the spotter in your team, and direct your fellow team members (shooters) to follow through with hitting the objective and achieving the desired result.

All results are based on your mission goals and targets.[56]

- Build a team that believes in focusing on the end result—the final target. If your team has to sell 100 cars by the end of the month, aim for 150!

---

56   Jim Kristoff, Goal Setting for Automotive Sales People, http://www.automotivedigitalmarketing.com/profiles/blogs/goal-setting-for-automotive-salespeople

- You must set metrics and match them to every single mission goal that you have. Remember your milestones? Each milestone needs goals and a set of metrics. What are your monthly sales ratios (e.g., new vs. used)? What is the appointment show ratio? Total amount of leads converted? Total amount of leads lost? Closing monthly conversion rate?

- In automotive digital strategy, it is not only about alignment but also about winning all of the small battles along the way. You will lose some of these battles almost certainly, but learning from them will give you an edge for the next campaign.

Every team member is a potential sniper. They should all be trained on their targets, waiting for their moment to strike and take action.

100 Days to Streamlining Your Strategy

It takes about 100 days to properly execute, analyze, and improve a specific digital strategy for your dealership. Within this, you may collect volumes of data on individual tactics, tweaks, and tips that need to become part of your team's overall knowledge base. And remember: You have to avoid rushing your digital strategy at all costs.

I have built and executed dozens of these strategies online, and each of them requires extreme focus, dedication, and ongoing commitment to improvement before, during, and after the strategy is complete. If you choose to rush your strategy for the sake of moving on to something else, you will run the danger of compromising your results and the success of your team.

When you send your special ops team into a battle zone and tell them after the drop they have half of the time to achieve the mission than they had prepared for, you can bet that disaster will rightly result. There are reasons why you create and deploy sometimes flexible plans and strategies and just can't stick to your roadmap, but believe me, rushing will not ever be one of them.

Spend a good 100 days in evaluating your current online entities and the approach of streamlining your current strategy.

- Conduct price checks, and schedule vendor meetings from anyone that is a third party and provides their services to you.
- Collect all of the metric data that you can; when possible, also from the traditional offline marketing activities.
- Compile volumes of competitor research (SWOT analysis).
- Determine if your current marketing operations are in a Crawl, Walk, or Run stage.
- What was done and tried digitally in the past, and why did it fail/succeed?
- What online channels were touched or not touched so far?
- What about social media? Who is posting what and how often? And why?
- Who provided the content of the websites?
- What processes are currently in place for the online sales team? For the floor sales team?
- What happens after a delivery?
- How is our reputation? What are our customers saying about us, and where can I find it?

As you can see, I could possibly fill another two pages of questions I would ask when taking over a new team and endeavor to revamp or create a digital strategy. I just discovered for myself that the 100 days are a very good time frame to get the gist out of what to expect.

A 100 day action plan will give you time to clarify your expectations, set your agenda, forge the right relationships, find new insights, structure the right team, develop the best strategy, then define the most adequate processes—while testing and measuring them along the way. You will build quality systems for success with this test-on-the-go (or should I say learning-by-doing) model.

Each stage of the buying journey must be audited, tested, and improved to perfection. This is how you gain the competitive advantage.[57]

Online Success and the Roman Analogy

Rome was not built in a day, and this rings true in the realm of automotive digital strategy as well. Too often teams blaze through their activities, gaining probably decent results but missing out on the opportunity to indeed own a market and their competition. They leapfrog over obstacles instead of finding viable solutions, and they distract themselves with easy-to-get results. Let me just call it as I see it: Sloppy!

Your online success will not happen in one day. It takes a dedicated leader and a team of professionals to conduct multiple strategies and campaigns to determine what works for your local or regional market. Every target demographic is different and every tactic is different, and this is why online strategy has leveled the playing field for so many smaller dealerships somewhere out in the pampa kicking bigger city car dealers in their behinds.

Keep in mind that you are in your enemy's backyard *all* of the time. Even though it may seem quiet, your direct competition is

57   Jeremy Alicandri, The Differential Advantages That Made Cobalt the "Elephant" of Automotive Digital Marketing, http://www.drivingsales.com/blogs/ jeremy/2013/11/13/the-differential-advantages-allowed-cobalt-to-become-elephant- automotive-digital-marketing

constantly watching you. They will capitalize on your mistakes and take advantage of your laziness. After each campaign—even though your troops will be tired and listless—you must debrief them.

This analogy pertains to how you treat your analytics. All ad and online campaigns will produce volumes of data that need to be combed through and analyzed—and worthy decisions must be made for the next round of campaign tests. Do this religiously, and this is how you eventually overwhelm your enemy and win the upper hand!

Online success belongs to the online marketer that can effectively conduct these strategies and campaigns while constantly measuring and improving their results.[58] As long as the team and the metrics are improving—and your targets are being hit—your team will become an unstoppable tactical force that is able to swoop in and sell hundreds of customers on demand.

One day, when a competitor rises and launches an attack on you, your team will have already seen it coming and have a response waiting. No one will be able to seize your market share. The best defense is a good offense—debrief, debrief, debrief.

How Compromise Leads to Cut Corners

As I have mentioned before, digital strategy should be flexible but not for the wrong reasons. Otherwise, you will have wasted your time putting together the strategy in the first place and will end up with a greatly diminished end result.

You as a leader need to lead by example and just cannot accept standards that are lower than desirable. Never compromise keeping the focus and the mission objectives alive or your team

---

58   Bjoern Mayland, Dr Thomas Heiland, Managing Variety on the Internet – Strategic Competitive Advantage in the Automotive Industry, http://www.wirtschaft. fh-dortmund.de/~ib/DIfEaIS/HTML/PDF/Mayland_Heiland.pdf

will learn that cutting corners is acceptable. It is sometimes very tempting to go for an easy win when there are more challenges out there that have to be explored. But exploration and discovery are the point because you are investing in human capital and your knowledge base.

It always begins, as I discussed in the chapters before, by picking the right team. Use teamwork and collaboration to your ultimate advantage. By having a plan, you can make sure to create and establish viable, measurable checkpoints to re-check, re-evaluate, and re-group. When you establish a process that allows you to know your enemy well, it will give you the preparation for any kind of attack. When you are at the point where you have figured out the best pick of your approach, which online strategy promises success, find the right weapons to use in battle and understand the vehicles that will drive this effort forward.

Once you have done all of these steps and have done them with razor-sharp focus—and without rushing any steps—you will gain online dominance and recognizable marketing success. I am not talking about the success that comes with a few more sold cars by the end of the month. I am talking about the kind of success that hails in a new era of marketing for your entire company and your dealership brand.

This is the kind of necessary takeover even your traditional marketing team or current ad agency will understand. They will get on board with you if you have repeatedly proven that the money and, even more importantly, accountability factor is in digital strategy. Metrics, analytics, data, targeted campaigns, faster churn, lower production costs, and flexibility—this is the "stuff" that will win you their respect while building cohesive teams that thrive in unpredictable consumer environments and acknowledge that the consumer journey has become more predictable and digital.

When your returns on investment[59] turn heads, that is when you will seal your team's victory. That is when you will succeed in the multiple campaigns and operations, and it will be also where your real challenges will begin, again and again.

---

[59] Revving Up Automotive Digital Marketing ROI, http://www.accenture.com/ SiteCollectionDocuments/PDF/Accenture-Revving-Up-Automotive-Digital-Marketing-ROI.pdf

section 6

DRIVING ALONG NEW PATHS TO SUCCESS: PRACTICAL ROUTES

CHAPTER 11

SEO, SEM, and Content Creation Vehicles

"The days of SEO being a game outsmarting algorithms are over. Today content strategy and valuable, sustainable strategies are essential, not just tricks and links."

ADAM AUDETTE,
CHIEF KNOWLEDGE OFFICER, RKG

When you and your team have your infrastructure in place and the plan has been set, all that remains is implementation. But there are so many paths to success in the world of online marketing, and it is a battle that never ends once begun.

If you are going to drive new success paths, you will need to take the practical routes to get there. That means learning as many useful tips and techniques as you can and keeping yourself informed about the latest tech, marketing, and strategic news so that you are able to have a complete victory in your market.

Sign up to be a community member of DrivingSales.com, AutomotiveDigitalMarketing.com, Dealerrefresh.com, KainAutomotive.com, Idea Exchange, and all the others that are doing a great job providing great content and even better answers when talking digital marketing in the automotive space.

Further, sign up for the newsletter of Digital Dealer, Auto Dealer Monthly, Industry Summit, NADA News, and Hard Facts by Potratz to hear the latest news and tips.

Google's Matt Cutts on SEO and Content

The first thing about online digital strategy that you should know is that it is governed by whatever rules and algorithm changes Google, Bing, and Yahoo decide to implement. These rules change all the time and are constantly updated to keep people guessing about how Google measures content value and ranks online properties.

Matt Cutts, one of Google's finest engineers and King of Content and SEO concern has said many things about SEO and content that you should be aware of before launching a new campaign. Take note of these to get better placement on Google. Do this, and your content will naturally rank well on other search engines anyway.

- Matt Cutts advocates for original, clear, and understandable content that causes engagement as social markers are one of the top ranking factors on Google.[60]

- Advertorials and other paid content techniques are getting cracked down on as the practice can often be unethical when not declared on the publication. Keep yours transparent, and make sure that you do not employ any black hat techniques.

---

60   Jennifer Slegg, Matt Cutts: Write Clear, Understandable Content, http://searchenginewatch.com/article/2331473/Matt-Cutts-Write-Clear-Understandable-Content

- Authority matters to Google, so if they deduce that you are an expert in something (because of your content), they will rank your sites a little higher than others.

- Carefully working with Google Analytics is a great way to minimize damage from hackers, spam, and other bad practices—and to avoid any link issues.

The Online World Post Panda, Penguin, and Hummingbird

The way that Google judges where your websites or content rank on its search engine depends on what its algorithm says. This very algorithm is updated often and has caused major upheavals for many companies using poor or weak online marketing techniques to make money in an unethical manner. Google will not stand for that.

Because of this, you as an online marketer should keep one eye on Google at all times. They are your main source of traffic and revenue, and any changes that come from them mean that your rankings will be affected. Different ranks mean different revenue, so take note!

- Panda was the first algorithm change and was launched February 23, 2011. The goal for this update was to showcase higher quality sites in the search results and demote sites of lesser quality. Content farms suffered as keyword stuffing, duplicate content, and stolen content was demonized. Bad links were penalized.

- Penguin was the second algorithm change, launched April 24, 2012. This update sought to correct unnatural backlinks that were giving some websites the edge in the search results. Unnatural links can no longer be beneficial as Google shifts towards earned ranking with consistent content.

- The latest huge algorithm update, Hummingbird, was launched September 26, 2013. Unlike the previous two updates, Hummingbird was a total overhaul—a whole new engine. The goal was for the search engine to better understand a user's query. Content that answers a user's queries is now ranking well online.[61]

The online world was once a place brimming with black hat SEO, bad links, bought ranking, and poor quality, duplicate, ad-laden content. Google has put a stop to all of that in the past four years. That is why there has been such a major shift to content marketing.

Google wants to provide people with the best service possible, which means that your content and online brand presence needs to be in line with their ideals. For a timeless strategy, always keep your customer in mind, enhance their experience, and concentrate on engagement and content—and you cannot go wrong.

I encourage you to check and even get more involved in "How Google Thinks About Search" and visit their web entities:

- **http://googlewebmastercentral.blogspot.com/**
- **http://insidesearch.blogspot.com/**
- **https://productforums.google.com/forum/#!forum/ webmasters**

And do not forget to check out their YouTube Channel showing hundreds of how tos:

- **https://www.youtube.com/user/GoogleWebmasterHelp**

---

61   Rachel Sprung, Pandas, Penguins, Hummingbirds, Oh My! How to Keep Up With the Latest SEO Trends, http://blog.hubspot.com/marketing/how-to-keep-up-seo-trends-ht

Bad Practices That Will Crush Your Progress

I have said before that the world of online SEO is constantly changing. The brands and dealerships that want to compete and do well will realize that there are rules and that these rules must be followed, or they risk serious penalties and perhaps even removal off the major search engines that drive all marketing revenue.

Avoid these bad practices in your daily marketing routines:

- *Guest blogging for SEO needs to be treated with caution.* The reputation of the blogger now matters more than ever, so only accept guest posts from people with impeccable reputations. Otherwise, Google will penalize you.[62] Make sure that your posts are relevant and that Google authority is taken into account.

- *Beware of optimizing your anchor content.* Anchor text with keywords were once the norm for SEO teams, but now they invoke the wrath of penalties. Instead, use naked URLs, branded URLs, and long phrase anchor text.

- *Focus on link quality, not link quantity, or Google will notice.* Do not buy links, or you are asking for trouble. Linkbuilding[63] is still alive and well, but now you need to make sure that your practices are ethical.

- *Keyword stuffing is a real problem, and Google hates it.* Do not stuff your content with keywords, especially long tail keywords. Instead, focus on creating high quality content

---

62   Amy Gesenhues, Keep Writing Quality Content: SEO Bloggers React to Matt Cutts' Claim "Guest Blogging Is Dead," http://searchengineland.com/seo-bloggers-say-keep-writing-quality-content-reactions-to-matt-cutts-claim-guest-blogging-is-dead-182199

63   Neil Patel, 5 SEO Techniques You Should Stop Using Immediately, http://www.quicksprout.com/2014/03/28/5-seo-techniques-you-should-stop-using-immediately/

that engages your reader. Never place keywords in invisible text, never rely on keyword meta tags, and use more than one search term per piece of content!

The bottom line with SEO in this shining new age is that you cannot buy good rankings any more. You have to earn them with good and unique content. That means avoiding these bad practices or Google will literally crush your progress by penalizing your content.

Google wants you to clean up your act and provide real content value for your communities. You need to be the information source that teaches as you promote so that real value is delivered to their users. This is the only way you will rank well in the future—quality!

Using Storytelling to Connect

Many experts are saying that storytelling is the new SEO. It is making a wonderful comeback online for anyone willing to listen and get involved. Because of Google's algorithm changes, this new "earned" form of content needs to be engaging, entertaining, and highly viral—but most of all, it has to attract loads of traffic to work.

Content marketers and digital strategists have been using the almost-lost art of storytelling to achieve greater conversion rates than ever thought possible. It is a complete shift from trying to trick the search engine into better rankings with technical SEO to earning the rankings with quality stories in your content. A full 360!

The bottom line is that it matters how long people hang around on your site, how many of those will convert into a lead, how many return, and if you have a real community there. Panda and Penguin demand that content is king and will reign for many years to come. Content that really engages uses different types of media presented to a specific audience.

Content that has high engagement rates is usually what gets this done. Your dealership will have to communicate your brand story to build communities around your various online channels. These communities will become the repeat revenue and engagement that you need to maintain a solid spot on Google.

Instead of push marketing, draw or pull your readers in with a good story. Communicate in a human manner, and really connect with your message. Do this by using real people or characters in your marketing, giving them a conflict, and then solving this conflict using powerful storytelling techniques.[64]

One of the masters of storytelling in the automotive industry is currently Subaru with their "They Lived" campaign, showing a horrible, twisted wreckage and what is left of the real car that was in an accident and not a prop. The characters in this ad (police man, junkyard worker) are pointing out during the commercial "They Lived" while showing an on-screen copy at the end stating "Subaru. Five 2014 IIHS top safety picks."

The extension of this reality theme was accompanied by an additional website featuring actual letters from Subaru drivers pointing out how their Subaru has helped them save their lives during accidents. You can also check out the impactful combination of traditional marketing (TV commercial) and online strategies (dedicated website/webpage) by visiting

http://www.subaru.com/why-subaru/livelove.html.

I think that makes the point clearer. Even greater than text-based storytelling for SEO and awareness is the new surge in visual storytelling that is transforming automotive ecommerce

---

64   Lauren Owens, The Elements of Good Storytelling & How You Can Use Storytelling in Marketing, http://www.morevisibility.com/blogs/seo/the-elements-of-good-storytelling-how-you-can-use-storytelling-in-marketing.html

departments into mini media companies. Using a variety of images and video, dealerships will now be able to create their own video media to connect and convert their audiences.

With my twenty years of business and marketing experience, I can honestly say that investing in multi-media SEO and storytelling techniques works. Google loves this engaging content, and it will help you spread your message to the right people at the right time.

How to Find The Right Content: Curating Success

Stories begin as ideas and then slowly become part of other people's content. To get new story ideas and find other quality content to share on your social platforms, you will have to learn to use the power of content curation. Defined, this is simply the act of collecting valuable content online with the intention of using it later in your own strategies. I have to admit, my favorite helper is the app "Pocket," which I have linked not only on my "Zite" news app but also use as an extension on my Chrome browser, allowing me to pick now and utilize later.

In this new battle for content superiority, you need to be aware that the companies with the latest, most reliable, and most relevant content win. That means it pays to constantly be on the hunt for new nuggets of content info. I like to think of it like a special ops game: as the soldiers are moving through the landscape, they stop to collect coins as rewards.

- *Set up Google Alerts using your most important keyword combinations.* If anything new has happened in this field, Google will email you with the list of the latest content titles that are ranking under this term. This is a great set-it-and-forget-it curation tactic.
- *Social networks are also excellent for curation.* Twitter, for example, has hashtag searches brimming with expert

content, quotes, and links to valuable blog posts and other free media. Use Facebook, Pinterest, YouTube, and the other networks to find niche-relevant content that leaps off the screen.

- *Make use of a curation engine by putting the right technology or tools in place.* This can be done using many multipurpose tools like Oktopost or Paper.li or my personal favorite, GetPocket , where you can curate as you search online and save everything in a secure, private backend for later review.

- *Do not underestimate how useful bookmarking tools are with sites like Digg, Reddit, and StumbleUpon still making the list of top content curators for your brand.* A lot of these sites have become indispensable for user-generated content as they inspire a lot of real world, real time engagement.

To curate success,[65] you will have to begin to search the Internet for valuable content and for places to store this content for use in your digital strategies. Put aside an hour every day to run through a curation practice or schedule so that you are integrating other voices and pieces of content into your own digital strategies.

Make sure you are using keywords in this strategy that are relevant for your purposes. For example, you want to be the #1 hybrid vehicle dealer in your DMA, so use words like "alternative fuel," "EV," MPG, and similar in your content curators and alerts to:

- Know what the latest in this niche is.
- Understand what would be ideal to share with your customers via website, blog, social, and email campaigns.

---

65   Christina McCale, Four Tactics to Curate Content the Right Way, http://www. elto.com/blog/four-tactics-to-curate-content-the-right-way/

Becoming a Blog Authority

Let's get something straight right from the beginning—bloggers rule the world of content online. They get the highest rankings because their content inspires the most engagement, sharing, and general hustle and bustle. Your brand and your team will need to have access to a blog authority or in-house blogger to create hot content for your dealership and the brands you sell.

Online authority will become *the* key performance indicator for all future digital strategies conducted on Google. They want you to become a thought leader on a specific topic in your field so that you can communicate this expert information to your target audiences—providing them with accurate search results and real value.

That means you will need to focus on quality, consistency, and a clear blog message or content strategy as part of your overall strategic online campaigns. For your team, it will count in your favor if you launch a blog that deals with everything car and brand related, and I do not mean to push sales via your sharings. Approach non-sales related subjects from a specific angle to make your blog original and valuable for your readers.

On this blog, share your adventures with the world by reporting on your challenges, like how difficult it is to keep Model ABC on the lot because of their raving reviews in the car magazines or to get off the smashed bugs on your windshield and grill after a summer night drive on the highway and by letting your community and potential buyers close to your blogger. They want to know who the face is behind the words to connect on an emotional level. People buy from other people, but most of all, they buy ideas. A good blogger can attract more store visitors and eventually sell more cars.

Once your online marketing dealership has broken into the field of authority blogging,[66] you will begin to get offers to trade posts and to guest post for some very large blogs in your niche. It happened to me in 2004 when I wrote for the German newspaper issued in Michigan on things like "European delivery and how beautiful Germany can be experienced when picking up your new Mercedes-Benz" or explaining what a new feature with the name of "Adaptive Cruise Control" (now known as distronic) can actually do for you during a long highway ride. Be yourself when writing, and lend your blog your real voice, exactly how you would speak if you explain something to a best friend. And no sales pitch whatsoever.

Expect to get a lot more SEO power with a genuinely talented blogger than with an SEO team. Unfortunately, content takes longer, and there are no short cuts—so plan to integrate your authority blog into your digital strategy soon so that your dealership can stay relevant, gather community weights, and, of course, get more customers to respond to you.

---

66   Jeff Goins, The Surprising Key to Becoming an Authority, http://goinswriter. com/authority-blog/

CHAPTER 12

Your Website Vehicle

"It's much easier to double your business by doubling your conversion rate than by doubling your traffic."

JEFF EISENBERG

O f all the online properties that will showcase your content, none is more important than your main website and the other microsites that are related to selling for your brand and dealership. You may have a blog and several different microsites, but the fact remains—fail to convert on your main URL, and you will not be pulling in much foot traffic or generating inbound phone calls or email inquiries.

Your website vehicles are therefore a critical part of your overall digital strategies. All marketing and advertising leads there, so you will want to spend a good amount of time making sure that you are getting the conversions that you deserve. This is how you erect a solid base of operations for your team—by making sure your infrastructure and message is always up to date.

Building Landing Page Campaigns

Inbound marketing is a type of marketing that focuses on attracting potential community members and leads to your sites. Instead of reaching out with cold calling, direct selling, and inaccurate marketing messages, you spend time attracting and converting leads to specific online properties, where methods can be measured and improved.

A landing page[67] is a web page that your visitor will "land on" after choosing to click on a call to action or marketing message. This standalone webpage is responsible for converting your lead into a sale, so it often contains no global navigation to contain that visitor. The two types of landing page are lead capture pages and click through pages. When taking Two Legits Agency's "Your 2014 Digital Marketing Road-Map" into account, they are talking about the fact that companies with 30 or more landing pages generate seven times more leads than those with fewer than 10.

With your average click through landing page, you are charged with directing visitors along the sales funnel by enticing them with a friendly and targeted pitch. This warms them up for the sale instead of simply leading them directly to a cart or a test drive booking, for example. The lead capture page does something similar except that it captures data like email addresses.

The goal is either for a direct appointment booking, a sales quote inquiry, or to capture emails for later conversion. A good landing page campaign cannot only attract a lot of traffic but also serves as highly qualified email leads collector tool. Your email marketing process will do the rest.

---

67   What Is a Landing Page?, http://unbounce.com/landing-page-articles/what-is-a-landing-page/

"Not Released" Vehicle Models on Detail Pages

In automotive digital strategy, OEM websites are considered the most informative (65%), followed by independent review sites (41%) and then dealership websites (38%), according to Nielson's Global Survey of Automotive Demand.[68] On your own websites, you should consider creating "not yet released", "future vehicles," or "up and coming" vehicle model pages that detail what is coming and can be expected in your showrooms.

These prelaunch pages will inspire your community, provoke discussion about the new cars, and lead to a lot more leads and eventual sales in your DMA. You want to make sure that you are indeed the trusted informant to your consumers and that you know what is up in your community and know and are willing to share all the facts before any competing dealerships around you would do so. People are always looking for the latest model, and these models are usually released with limited information. Be a real journalistic brand and research what you can say about the upcoming releases.

Few digital dealers take the time to acknowledge the benefits of pre-promoting cars that have not been released yet. Then there are the concept cars that will never be released. All of these attract fans and conversation—and they convert into more sales for your brand. Do not underestimate the long sale, as these can add up over time.

I remember when in 2009 the all-new BMW Z4 began to roll out to the dealerships. The hype was huge considering BMW finally had considered giving the first time launched Z4 in 2003 a drastic make over and got rid of the canvas top for a hard-top

---

68   Nielson: 65% of Global Online Consumers Plan To Buy a New or Used Car In The Next Two Years, Online Advertising And Information Most Helpful For Buyers, http://www.nielson.com/us/en/press-room/2014/nielsen-65-of-global-online-consumers-plan-to-buy-a-new-or-used-car-in-the-next-tw-years.html

convertible roof. Even though there was enough information out in the BMW communities and Autoblogs, I wanted to provide my Atlanta BMW fans with a bit more.

One morning coming to work, the car transporter had just arrived a couple minutes prior. On it were two brand-spanking new BMW Z4s in white and blue. I parked my car in the middle lane of the street, just in front of the transporter, jumped out of the car, had my FlipCam in hand, and started filming and speaking on "how excited I was...and and and..." even before the cars were unloaded. After two minutes I ran into my office, downloaded the footage immediately onto our dealership's YouTube channel, chose the headline "First 2009 BMW Z4 hard-top Roadster hits Atlanta, Georgia," linked the YouTube URL to our 2009 BMW Z4 detail page, which I had initiated five months earlier on our dealer website and showed and shared until this date spy pictures, German pics on the Z4, etc., and finally embedded the first live Z4 video made by a dealer in Georgia on my BMWAtlantaBlogger WordPress blog. Two hours later I went again to the car, now PDIed, and videotaped how beautiful the mechanics work when letting down the hard-top roof into the trunk by just using the BMW key. Again, onto YouTube and the Z4 Vehicle Page on our website and blog.

Results: After just seven days, we had more than 18,000 views on the YouTube channel (more than the then official BMW OEM channel had on this car), numerous comments, the blog visits spiked by +110% for this week, and our Z4 detail page on our BMW homepage was the second most visited page for the month.

A lot of the time, if your dealership wants to sell a few more of these new releases, it is going to take a considerable push for action on your part. These detail pages can help you collect pre-orders, book test drives, and get people into your showroom floor on the day that the car is launched.

Blogging, when I did it early in 2007 for the dealership, was still sometimes triggering "why would you do that" questions from my peeps. But I figured out early on that digital strategy is all about the experience you want to provide to your customers and the community involved in your service and cars. It takes commitment and passion for your "job" and the brand you want to see thrive. So make your experiences worth waiting for.

Keep in mind that during Hubspot's State of Inbound Marketing in 2012, it was discovered that 92 percent of companies that considered maintaining a blog multiple times during a day had acquired a customer through their blog. So did we for our dealership!

It is also useful to point out that when this exclusive content is placed on your website, it keeps people there for longer, improving several critical website metrics used to determine the authority and value of a website for Google ranking purposes. Your website will rise through engagement and authority in the search engines when your fans stay to browse on your "coming soon" model pages.

Large Images on Inventory Pages: The Stats

There is a good amount of evidence to indicate that the rising trend in visual marketing is key to unlocking a lot of new business for your dealership. Your vehicle images on your websites have always been important, but a 2014 Inventory Shopping Experience Study[69] conducted by Cobalt proves that stock photos leave people with a negative impression.

The feeling is that stock images lead people to believe that the cars are "all the same," and because nothing stands out for them, a much lower click through rate results. Considering your vehicle

---

69   Eye Candy...How Stock Photos Can Kill a Vehicles Love Life, http://www.dealerrefresh.com/stock-new-car-photos-vs-actual-photos/

detail pages are where much of the conversion magic happens, this is an unacceptable statistic for your digital strategy.

Another study conducted by Kelley Blue Book Marketing Research[70] found that 90% of vehicle shoppers prefer to see actual "new" car photos of the exact vehicle that they could potentially own instead of standard stock images.

To facilitate this process on an even bigger scale, evidence supports the idea that larger product images on inventory pages tend to have more engagement and create higher numbers of call-to-action. I am not talking about the click to enlarge image function; I am talking about larger images directly on the VDP as a default.

In a case study where Traffic4U[71] conducted multivariate testing for Hyundai, one of the metrics to test for was larger images. Their goal was to get more bookings for test drives, and it was hugely successful. The MVPs in these tests were the larger car images, as they enticed the potential buyer to commit to viewing the car.

How Color Influences Buyer Behavior

There is real science behind the "art" of design and applying color to your automotive digital marketing techniques. The teams that learn to harness the power of color will have more success over time as they apply these universal principles to different campaigns.

Consumers place an enormous amount of emphasis on visual appearance when shopping around for products or information related to products online. Of all the senses, it is our visual

---

70   Kim Essenmacher, Do New Car Photos Really Make a Difference From Stock Photos, http://www.automotivedigitalmarketing.com/forum/topics/do-new-car-photos-really-make-a-difference-from-stock-photos

71   How Hyundai Increased Requests for Test Drive by 62% Using Multivariate Testing, https://vwo.com/blog/multivariate-testing-case-study/

sense that works best with online marketing. That is why social networks like Pinterest have sprung up over the last few years— images deliver messages at a glance.

To influence your potential buyers and leads, you must understand how color plays a role in the psychology of online purchasing. Consider the follow stats:

- 85% of shoppers[72] say that color is the primary reason that they buy a particular product. That means the car colors that you choose to display may influence how many CTAs you get from your website.

- Color is also directly related to brand recognition, improving it by 80% and increasing consumer confidence in your brand or product.

- Different colors say different things about your campaign. Blue represents trust and security (Volvo, Subaru), green represents wealth and nature (Land Rover, Jeep), red represents energy and urgency (Audi), yellow represents youth and optimism (Lotus), black is about power and luxury (Lamborghini), and purple represents calm and beauty (take a look at the Infiniti website).

The colors that you choose to use in your digital marketing campaigns will affect the mood, attitude, and attention span of your consumer. The way you use these colors can improve your overall conversion rates if you test to see which colors work best with your various materials and pitches.

Creating a blue-themed blog, for example, may get you more credibility and trust early on, which will pass traffic on to your native dealer sites.

---

72   How Do Colors Affect Purchases?, http://blog.kissmetrics.com/color-psychology/

Working With Call to Action Opportunities

A call to action is self-explanatory, and yet it is an element in online selling that is often overlooked, ignored, or misused. Finding the right call to action for your various websites depends on what you want people to do there.

A simple click through can be motivated in a friendly manner with a text-based hook like "click here for more," but often it is the unique, personalized calls to action that make the most impact. This requires communicating your brand tone through your call to action buttons so that consumers or leads really feel like they are investing in you and not just another random button connecting to a landing page.

- A good call to action inspires action[73]; it does not demand it. Make it a simple, clear, one-step process so that no confusion results.
- Always give your consumer a very good reason why they should click on a button or call to action. "You will never believe how much torque BMW packed into their latest two-door sedan. Click here for in-depth specs on the car!"
- Your call to action should not melt into your landing page. It needs to stand out and be visually appealing to be clicked on. Think "contrast." In fact, if you can make the button impossible to not click on, that would be great. Design and use color to your advantage here.
- Include at least two CTAs on your homepage and above the fold.

Call to action opportunities should always be split tested, in my opinion, to make sure that you are getting the most out of your

---

73   Paul Potratz, What's Your Call to Action?, http://www. automotivedigitalmarketing.com/profiles/blogs/what-s-your-call-to-action

webpages and are accommodating the needs of your consumer's journey. Fact is, a CTA button needs to literally make action happen.

Driving Metrics: The Bounce and Exit Rate

A big part of any performance-based digital marketing strategy hinges on the metrics that you produce there. If you do not know how effective your marketing messages are, then you will not be able to improve them. That means you need to keep an eye on the key performance indicators for each campaign.

To drive your metric goals forward, make sure that you identify and align your metrics with your dealership's branding objectives before any new strategy or campaign. Your analytics are your insurance policy for measuring how successful every element has been on your webpage. With basic testing, you are able to find out how many views your website has received, how long people stayed on which page, when they bounced and left each page, and so much more.

A bounce rate[74] is a metric on a web page that measures the percentage of visitors that hit your website on a specific page and do not visit any of your other web pages. Landing pages are measured by bounce rate, and it matters how high it gets. A high bounce rate means that people are not sticking around to be converted on that page.

A bounce rate is an excellent measure of the quality of traffic being attracted to your site. On a landing page, you need to aim for a low bounce rate, which will prove that your leads are staying on the page to consume your marketing message and hopefully take action—whether it is to sign up for an email list or book a test drive.

---

74   Avinash Kaushik, Standard Metrics Revisited: #3: Bounce Rate, http://www.kaushik.net/avinash/standard-metrics-revisited-3-bounce-rate/

When your bounce rate is low, it means that your landing page visitors may have continued on from that page to other pages on your website. If it is high, it means that too many visitors left your website shortly after arriving on the landing page.

An exit rate is the percentage of visitors that leave your site from any other page based on the number of visits to that specific page. Each page has its own exit rate, and again, these need to be as low as possible.

Keep a close eye on these two metrics to maintain the integrity of your page content and marketing message. Playing around with them will help you improve your page conversions beyond the 1-2% mark. Every page inside your dealer website will be different, so do not apply the same rules across all pages. Test, test, and test again!

CHAPTER 13

Tribes and Social Marketing Vehicles

"A tribe is a group of people connected to one another, connected to a leader, and connected to an idea. For millions of years, human beings have been part of one tribe or another. A group needs only two things to be a tribe: a shared interest and a way to communicate."

SETH GODIN

In this chapter, you will get a rundown of what it means to build a tribe around specific social channels for promotion and unique marketing opportunities. Social marketing vehicles can be considered as some of the most interesting conversion tools for your dealership and brand.

The main objective for many of these social platforms is not just to feed your website's traffic and increase your brand awareness but it is also to help you convert fans into brand advocates, a much stronger form of fan that uses word-of-mouth marketing to get you more sales.

The Six Main Tribes to Nurture

There are few battlefields quite like the social battlefield online, which is made up of at least six key areas or properties. This is where you will send your troops and where many of your marketing practices will be conducted. This is where your brand will build your own tribes.

Tribe marketing is when you market for the benefit of your leads or community, not just to sell cars. Experiential marketing is a sub sect of this as a form of advertising that focuses on helping consumers experience a brand and what they are all about.[75] There are six main tribes that you will need to nurture for repeat sales.

1. *Facebook:* Build your community on Facebook for consistent repeat sales and the chance to promote to lots of fans that genuinely love your brand or dealership. Eighty-two percent of consumers say that this is a good place to interact with brands. [76]

2. *Twitter:* Twitter is a micro-blogging platform that is superb for live events, updates, news, and link sharing. It should be part of your digital strategies at all times considering that 44% of marketers reported having acquired customers out of Twitter.

3. *LinkedIn:* This business social network gives you access to other experts, so make influencer connections there, engage in groups, or run your own group for leads. And always keep this in mind: around 64% of all visits from social media channels to corporate websites are being generated from here.

---

75   Experiential Marketing 101: What Is Experiential Marketing?, http://www. creativeguerrillamarketing.com/guerrilla-marketing/experiential-101-experiential-marketing/

76   http://www.marketingtechblog.com/2014-digital-marketing-roadmap/

4. *Pinterest:* An image social network, Pinterest has the highest click through rates of any other social network, and it can get you a lot of fresh leads. Who knows? You may even be a part of the 21% of users that see a product here and then purchase it.

5. *Instagram:* A great image sharing network, Instagram photos are highly viral, and people love seeing cars in this format. Build your community here.

6. *Google+:* This is Google's response to Facebook, but it is an SEO tool of note. This social network is excellent at sharing multiple media formats and displaying unique videos to the "friends" of circles and their different kinds of interests.

Content Types and Posting Schedules

Your automotive digital strategy should contain many different types of media content for dissemination among your various social platforms. Knowing when to post and which types of content get the best conversions on that platform will help you sell more cars.

- On Facebook[77] the best time to post is on weekdays, but the best times to engage are on Thursdays and Fridays. Studies have found that engagement is also 32% higher on weekends because people have more time to explore their favorite social network.

- The best time to tweet for engagement (clicks, comments, likes, shares) also seems to be on the weekend, although evidence suggests that posts at 6 p.m. from Monday through to Friday get higher click through rates.

---

77   Leo Wildrich, The 7 Most Interesting Social Media Studies and What to Learn From Them, http://blog.bufferapp.com/social-media-stats-studies

- Blog posts should be published in the morning—with 70%[78] of users saying that they read blogs at this time of day. Mondays in particular are great days for blog posting.
- The best time to post updates and video and image content on Google+ is on weekdays between 9 and 11 a.m. Likewise, LinkedIn is used most often just before and just after work and mostly on Tuesdays and Thursdays.
- Pinterest enjoys greater engagement rates on Saturday mornings between 2 and 4 p.m. and 8–11 a.m. The worst times to post on Pinterest are just after work or in the early hours of the morning.
- On Instagram, off hours seem to be the best between 9 p.m. and 8 a.m.[79] This is when videos are engaged with most often.

Of course, take these suggestions with a grain of salt considering none of these has been tested for your particular DMA or model; this is something you will have to do to get accurate posting times to match with particular content. You will need to undergo a benchmarking process, where you test out your posting times and draft a guide to posting for greater engagement for your dealership or brand.

The Important Role of Social Monitoring in Sales

In sales, you can learn a lot about your target demographic by listening to what they are saying about your company or brand online. But this requires your team to build in a social monitoring practice for a few hours every week.

---

78   Belle Beth Cooper, A Scientific Guide to Posting Tweets, Facebook Posts, Emails, and Blog Posts at the Best Time, http://blog.bufferapp.com/best-time-to-tweet-post-to-facebook-send-emails-publish-blogposts

79   The Best Time of Day to Post on Instagram, http://trackmaven.com/blog/2013/09/the-best-time-of-day-to-post-on-instagram/

In old school military situations, there was always a guy that had a two-way radio strapped to his back to reach headquarters and hear any important news or information that may influence their mission progress on the ground. That is what social monitoring is for you and your team today. Listen to your market, and watch out for your competitors.

This is easily done by employing the use of some savvy social monitoring tools. Hootsuite will collect your social media analytics and create reports for you, while other tools, like Social Mention, Buffer, or Sprout Social, will keep you updated on the stats about your content progress. Finding the right tools will make this part of your job easier.

For car dealerships and their brands, social monitoring of what is said about the customer's perception after picking up the car from service or feelings they experienced during the negotiation process when buying a car is critical to all sales and profit centers inside the dealership and dealer group. It contributes to your ongoing market intelligence pursuits and will help you maintain brand loyalty across all of your social media and reputation or review platforms. This also means you create a greater customer engagement, more effective one-on-one communication and competitive monitoring, and—at the end of it all—more happy customers and sales personnel and happier bosses of yours too.

With tools like Boardtracker, Google Alerts, Addict-o-Matic, and Technorati,[80] you can keep track of consumer sentiment about your name, brand, franchise, what they want from you, what they do not like from you, and what media is influencing their purchasing decisions.

When you take the time to listen in on what your consumers want, you will rapidly benefit from it. Monitoring is not a passive

---

80   Benefits of Social Media Monitoring for Auto Dealers, http://www.slideshare. net/wikimotive/benefits-of-social-media-monitoring-for-auto-dealers

practice; it is an active one that should be conducted for at least 15 minutes a day by your selected social media person or a great third party vendor. When you know what they are doing and they provide you with reports and alerts, you may get to engage with a consumer immediately and handle possible negative feedbacks received.

This is how you insert yourself into conversations and convert negative experiences, hopefully, into positive ones while enhancing the way your consumers feel about your company and team. Avoiding answering or addressing any negative sentiment or even trying to be a smartass with a complainant will get you nowhere. The old school formula "The customer is King but I am the Emperor" or "all buyers are liars" will not fly any longer. Admit your wrongdoing, and even when you know that the consumer just "slammed" you in the social sphere or any of the numerous review sites, engage with them politely and tell her or him "Thank you for bringing the matter to my attention. We are truly sorry that you felt this way, and I can promise that we are in the process of reviewing our internal process to cut out any future mishaps. I would like to offer you to contact me (GM/GSM) directly at phone number xxx (do not write down the switchboard but your desk phone number) so that we can make sure your concerns are all addressed. Thank you." Do not miss out on the chance to incorporate some real time lessons into your strategy.

Using Social Ads, Stats, and Trends to Sell

Social networking is all about finding and connecting with the right audiences. When you use these social platforms, you are able to collect stats and recognize trends that are directly related to your actual consumer base and needs instead of having to rely on general reports from large research companies like we had to do back in the nineties.

According to a comScore Action Lift study,[81] automotive campaigns on Facebook drive more people to consider brands and models advertised, and they decrease competitor consideration. That means more visits to your brand's dealer websites and better conversions. Facebook in particular is excellent for social advertising because consumers can be targeted accurately.

The more you know about your target demographics from your websites and social media channels—and from your OEM's market research—the more you can apply it to social advertising campaigns to appeal to a specific market segment at the right time of day. This drastically improves conversions and eventually leads to greater numbers of vehicles sold.

The result of the comScore study determined that Facebook campaigns for the auto industry tend to enhance mid-funnel performance. This can be translated into serious conversions if you take the time to map out the data you collect from your Facebook insights analytics over time and then apply the buyer persona knowledge to the social ad filters.

Social ads can be used to enhance your social data on any of the social networks that you plan on using to build effective online communities. Mazda, for example, just launched a new microsite at the end of July 2014 that unveiled the new 2016 MX-5 Miata Roadster. From this microsite, several social campaigns are tied into it. Next to video content on MX-5's performance, you will also see interviews with the band Duran Duran to associate the nostalgia element with the car, considering it debuted first in 1989, when Duran Duran's "The Reflex" appeared on the vast majority of Walkmans playing all over the world.

Further, music played during the TV show *Fashion Rocks* will unlock additional Mazda content when using the Shazam app. To

---

81   Driving Brand and Vehicle Consideration Online, https://fbcdn-dragon-a. akamaihd.net/hphotos-ak-prn1/851584_648931531814771_180904602_n.pdf

round out the entire campaign, additional Facebook, Twitter, and Instagram content are included. Keep in mind that an effective social media tactical plan needs to be created to keep all of your properties populated with content that can then be enhanced with the target ad campaign processes.

In Mazda's case, they used additional digital marketing assets with AOL Networks with banner ads and creative content on Huffington Post and Stylist to reroute more online traffic back to the microsite.

When you begin to sort through the metric data and compile practical reports for effective decision-making for future social media combined with your digital online campaigns that work, you will quickly realize how valuable the advertising tools are that these sites offer. You can indeed gather a lot of real fans—and hopefully soon "brand evangelists"—and the desired lead conversions with social advertising.

Working With Top Consumer Review Sites

In the game of creating brand advocates that will support your campaigns, share your content, and mention positive things about your dealership online, in order to maintain a quality reputation, you will need to have some kind of consumer review relationship with websites like Cars.com, DealerRater.com, and Yelp.

When a fan has an excellent brand experience and decides that your ideals align with theirs, they will want to leave a great review for you. Brand advocates are not silent participants; they are always active and eager to spread your gospel online.

Directing these individuals to your consumer review sites will help your brand build a quality reputation by generating tons of four- or maybe even five-star reviews. Remember how critical reviews are to new consumer opinion? Brand advocates will pass on the torch and make sure that you continue to get new consumers that will also appreciate the way you run your dealership. Keep in mind that conversion rates can be four to 10 times higher for offers coming from trusted advocates.

With today's mobility—meaning here the instant connectivity of our smart phone devices—all customers have become online critics, with social media and consumer review site apps on the mobile screen and fuelling their sentiment. The irony is that it takes a strong emotion to get someone to leave a review, which means that if you are not actively recruiting brand advocates, you easily running the danger of a lot of negative reviews finding their way to these review pages.

Smart brands recruit early on these so called brand advocates or evangelists by not only providing first class consumer experiences but also including them early on in things such as beta tests, exclusive launches, pre-peek events, etc. By using this kind of army of brand advocates as viable back-up reserve troops against negative sentiment online from the odd "wronged" customer, you are able to level the playing field. Even if you have the best car dealership in the area, you will possibly never have 100% positive reviews, and this is good. I rather would have 4.7 or 4.8 stars out of a possible 5 stars because that makes you appear "human" for people reading these review sites. Remind yourself that "nobody is perfect," and tell your group "...but we are striving for the most possible term of 'perfect,'" which 4.8 stars could certainly stand for.

Monitoring these third party review sites needs to be on your weekly list of to-dos. Someone on your team has to watch out for negative sentiment,[82] address it, and make sure that it does not escalate to social networks. This is what I mean by working with top consumer review sites—so make sure that you have this covered in your digital strategy.

---

82   Don't Let Bad Reviews Slow You Down: Automotive Business and Car Dealership Review Sites to Monitor, http://www.reviewtrackers.com/dont-bad-reviews-slow-down-automotive-business-car-dealership-review-sites-monitor/

Retention Strategies and Producing Brand Advocates

One of the best retention strategies that you can use is to take customer experience to the next level and convert fans into brand advocates. These evangelists can do far more for your brand than your sales team, and you do not have to pay them to do it. When a brand advocate is happy, they will go out of their way to promote for your brand.

According to Rob Ruggetta, brand advocates are 50%[83] more influential than an average customer. These fan leaders help you perform the following critical practices:

- They spread word of mouth marketing, which accelerates your growth. Friends, colleagues, and people on social media will love hearing unbiased, third party promotion from these pleased customers.

- They increase your brand awareness. Spreading the word about your brand becomes second nature to them, and whenever they get the chance, they will say positive things to hold your dealership brand up high.

- They have lots of loyalty and increased lifetime value. Brand advocates will often be very loyal to your dealership, buying only from you. They will also get everyone around them to see that buying from you is always best. They inspire others to be brand advocates and to become repeat customers.

A good retention strategy keeps existing customers coming back for more. A great one turns many customers into brand evangelists so that they can go out into the world and spread your brand message for you. There are always stories to tell—share

---

83   What Are Brand Advocates? Why Are They Important, http://blog. clientheartbeat.com/brand-advocates/

yours, provide them with unique VIP experiences, and watch as they bring in more business.

It should be your team's goal to convert all customers into brand advocates. This is, of course, easier said than done, but using the right approach, tools, and vehicles, you can make it happen. Build a quality retention strategy with your team to keep your reputation solid online and people hearing excellent things about your company.

CHAPTER 14

Video and Mobile Marketing Vehicles

"If you're not using mobile marketing to attract new customers to your business, don't worry— your competitors are already using it and are getting those customers instead."

JAMIE TURNER

ome of the best vehicles that you can use in your automotive digital strategies include those that contain video and mobile technologies. Organizing events and amplifying them using these innovative media options is a nice way to focus your converged media campaigns and make some real money from digital strategy.

Physical events need to be tied to the online world, and no media does this better than video and mobile campaigns. Learn how to use these sources to deliver your brand message, recruit brand advocates, and sell more cars off the showroom floor.

Your Vehicle YouTube Strategy

Any special ops team worth their salt knows how to conduct successful YouTube strategies. These video strategies can be simple, or they can be part of an integrated media campaign that uses multiple forms of media and platforms for delivery, just as I had described earlier on the Mazda MX-5 example.

YouTube is brilliant for social media marketing and SEO, and it has a huge variety of uses for a digital strategy team that wants to sell more cars on a smaller budget. Consumers love video, and all of your branding videos should be run through your YouTube channel.

- Create mini commercials[84] for your brand on a low budget, and reap the benefits of views, engagement, and higher SEO rankings.
- Establish personal and visual connections with your fans, consumers, and brand advocates by using video to respond to queries, to create modern FAQs, and to guide people that want to learn more about your processes.

In April 2013[85] more than a quarter of all branded videos on YouTube were shared within the first three days of launch. This doubled to 42% in 12 months and 65% within a week. Videos are excellent for short-term promotions because they make a long-term impact.

Plus, videos increase people's understanding of your product or service by 74%,[86] and 75% of people viewing videos visit the brand's website after they have seen it on YouTube. That means YouTube is a lead generation tool you cannot afford to leave out of your campaigns.

---

84   How to Create a YouTube Channel as Part of Your Car Dealer Marketing Strategy, http://yeschant.com/blog/how-to-create-a-youtube-channel-as-part-of-your-car-dealer-marketing-strategy/

85   Christopher Ratcliff, 15 Quick Tips or a Successful YouTube Strategy, https://econsultancy.com/blog/64882-15-quick-tips-for-a-successful-youtube-strategy

86   Sarah Mincher, 25 Amazing Video Marketing Statistics, http://www.digitalsherpa.com/blog/25-amazing-video-marketing-statistics/

Video Pre-Roll Options

Personally, I believe that YouTube pre-roll adverts are some of the best advertising investments that you can make online. Pre-roll ads are the adverts that pop up before you watch a YouTube video that you have chosen from the list. You may know it as a "skip ad" because that is what you click!

A pre-roll advert is powerful because it is an authentic type of interruptive advertising. It is used mainly to raise awareness[87] for your brand and can also be used for some incredible lead generation campaigns if you are creative and approach it from an engagement standpoint. Let's just be clear: no traditional, boring ads work on YouTube.

In automotive digital strategy, YouTube pre-roll ads have merit because they are low cost, and they are also highly geolocation targeted thanks to the fact that Google owns YouTube. Reach your ideal target demographic by segmenting your audience by interests, language, topics, geography and demographic.

These adverts can be short, take barely any investment and can be used for car-specific launches to drive traffic to your website if you are running contests or a particular promotion—or simply to get your dealership name out there.

This kind of display advertising is the best by far, and people are used to it thanks to generations of television advertising standards. You get all the benefits of the huge viewership with none of the hefty price tags.

---

87   Brian Carter, Why YouTube Pre-Roll Ads Rock & How to Take Advantage of Them, http://www.convinceandconvert.com/content-marketing/why-youtube-pre-roll-ads-rock-how-to-take-advantage-of-them/

- Pre-roll videos are also twice as effective[88] as banner ads, according to YuMe and Decipher in their latest joint study.

Other YouTube ad options include InStream ads that can be run mid-roll or post-roll depending on your choice. You can choose to use their banner and display ads too. These InStream ads can be skipped, or you can pay to have them play.

Stats and Trends in YouTube Marketing

According to a study released by the Kelsey Group, some 33%[89] of car dealers are currently taking advantage of online video on their websites. The same study suggested that 59% of the tested dealers plan to use video on their websites within 12 months. That was seven years ago! Today, most car dealerships can no longer avoid having a YouTube or video marketing campaign.

In 2014 YouTube has experienced an explosion of on-demand and over-the-top television with significantly more users watching via their tablets and phones. Online video users are expected to double to 1.5 billion by 2016.[90]

Digital reports that two billion videos are viewed every week that are monetized on YouTube, and for every auto-tweet shared, there are six new YouTube browsing sessions.[91] That means that video causes increased rates of sharing and discovery when used in conjunction with other social networks in integrated campaigns.

The latest YouTube trend has been about humanizing your brand and using personalities to connect with your audience;

88   Study: Pre-Roll Video Ads Are More Than Twice as Effective as Banner Ads, http://www.businessinsider.com/sc/pre-roll-is-more-effective-than-banner-ads-2013-11

89   Mark Robertson, Car Dealers Embrace Online Video – Automotive Online Video Marketing Trends, http://www.dealerrefresh.com/car-dealers-embrace-online-video/

90   Jeffery Hayzlett, Why Video Marketing Is Key in 2014, http://hayzlett.com/blog/why-video-marketing-key-2014/

91   Giselle Abramovich, 15 Stats Brands Should Know About Online Video, http://digiday.com/brands/celtra-15-must-know-stats-for-online-video/

for example, Kia and the just concluded 2014 Soccer World Cup in Brazil. With their ad "Football vs. Futbol," KIA used Brazilian Top Model and Victoria Secret Angel Adriana Mila as their spokesperson, making it clear that football is indeed futbol and wrapped up more than 3.3 million views on this particular YouTube Video. Two more YouTube ads with her accumulated another two million views. When comparing these Adriana Mila ads with the parallel running "Become a Fan" ad, featuring Kia's Optima Ltd driving through suburbia, the results are pretty much clear. Kia's Optima ad had just 24,435 views in the same time frame. Humanizing your brand can win you more recognition, hype, buzz and, in the best case scenario, conversion.

This revolves around the use of data and video performance as online marketing dealers are constantly trying to improve on their previous campaigns by combing through their video data for nuggets of insight.

By analyzing your data, you can spot niche-specific trends and devise new YouTube campaigns based on what your specific audience wants and on their behaviors and habits. Doing this will increase your conversions, and you will get more clicks to your website and more leads to your various landing pages and microsites. Focus on your views, traffic sources, engagement, referrals, and audience retention and conversions to see what you are doing wrong—or right.

In the future, the car dealerships that realize they have access to their "own television channel," at a low cost, will retain more clientele and conversion.

Advertising Strategies for Automotive Sales

More and more, people are accessing your websites using their phones and mobile devices. In fact, mobile devices have already overtaken desktop use. With this logic, you should be planning bigger and better mobile marketing ad strategies so that your dealership brand can take full advantage of the shift.

Your entire digital strategy team requires serious training with mobile marketing because advertising on these mobile platforms is no longer the future; it is now. Here are a few ways that you can ramp up your ad strategies using mobile technology.

- Text message marketing is simple to use and low cost, and some 99% of all text message[92] respondents open and read their messages. Improve your customer support by sending follow up text messages or text ad blasts for promotions.

- Build a mobile app for a specific campaign, and use it to gather valuable data on your users and consumers.

- Use technology with your apps, like QR codes, to lead car consumers not only to your campaign landing pages or for showcasing videos but also to adapt new ideas and innovations on how to use QR codes better. Mercedes-Benz, for example, created their campaign, "Rescue Assist," which will help first responders in locating the vehicle's structural information, like placement of batteries and airbags and information for performing a safe rescue. Since 2013 these QR codes have been installed in all vehicles during production.

- Look into the augmented reality apps and how to place consumers inside the car of their dreams. Audi has started this already. With use of their Audi eKurz Info App (kurz = short) for the European model, Audi A1, they showed that printed manuals are a thing from the past. By developing a newer app for the new Audi A3, the driver can now recognize up to 300 individual elements of the A3 with the lens of his

---

92   Derek Johnson, SMS Open Rates Exceed 99%, http://www.tatango.com/blog/sms-open-rates-exceed-99/

smart phone camera, which then returns relevant how-to information or virtual and animated 3-D layovers onto the phone screen. Welcome to the future of maintenance and owner manuals.

- Create a mobile website and app with a loyalty service rewards program that automatically checks in the driver when approaching the dealership. This is already happening at vendors that are using the Square Payment App. For example, when I pass the neighborhood coffee shop, my phone buzzes me and tells me that I can now pay for my coffee right away and virtually checks me in.

These new and advanced advertising strategies are excellent alternatives, especially when you use them in conjunction with other integrated media and OEM cross promotion strategies. You will love the data that you get, as you will be able to pinpoint what kind of car your buyers or service customers love simply by analyzing the data.

Successful Mobile Automotive Campaigns

Auto brands lead the charge when it comes to effective mobile marketing campaigns. You only need to recall a few wildly successful ones to realize the impact a single mobile campaign can have on your short- and long-term objectives.

- The Lexus "Create Amazing" mobile app[93] was a smash success. After experiencing trouble with their European market, the app sought to share insight with their new consumer base to help people reassess what they needed from a car. The mobile site converted users by allowing them to download brochures, book test drives, and review

---

93   Lexus – Creating Amazing, http://www.thinkwithgoogle.com/campaigns/lexus-lexus-creating-amazing.html

content that was specially created. High conversion rates abounded!

- Chevrolet, for their Chevy Game Time app, which was an occasion specific app that was meant to enhance a Super Bowl ad viewing experience, used converged media. The app was an aggressive marketing tactic that was used to distract viewers from other car ads that were showing on the day by offering them trivia based on their commercial. Right answers were placed in a draw to win a Chevy Sonic. With over 700,000 downloads, this mobile strategy was a smash success.

- Volkswagen's "Rock 'n Scroll" mobile app was massively innovative—using HTML5, websockets, geolocation, and Twitter to create a brand story for the Beetle, the likes of which people had never seen before. Instead of creating a video, they inspired their fans to create Volkswagen videos and upload them via their mobile phones—which caused a massive outbreak of virality.

- Renault launched a highly targeted mobile campaign recently focusing on their electric car. The mobile campaign uses multiple data sources combined with demographic and socio-economic data to reach their true fans. The ads[94] were displayed to these genuinely interested parties after they visited car dealership websites. The messages would appear within a five-mile radius of a Renault dealership, which was very smart.

Manufacturers and dealerships have already experienced massive success using mobile technology in a host of exciting ways. Make sure that your team is ready to do the same as mobile

---

94   Chantal Tode, Renault Launches Highly Targeted Mobile Campaign Targeting Electric Car Enthusiasts, http://www.mobilemarketer.com/cms/news/advertising/17870.html

brings together multiple types of media and allows you to get really creative with the way that your consumer receives their brand experience.

The Latest Trends and Stats in Mobile Marketing

Mobile marketing is the pinnacle of digital strategy at the moment. It unites all forms of rich media and delivers endless opportunities for creative teams that are desperate for real engagement and high conversions to make those critical sales.

According to Google, 26% of consumer journeys begin on a mobile application or website. If you do not have a branded app just yet, perhaps the time is right to consider one before your competitors realize you are not capitalizing on modern technology.

The verdict is in—some 89%[95] of media time is spent on mobile apps, not mobile websites. People seem to prefer it when you build a platform specifically for use on a mobile device. Heidi Cohen reports[96] that there are now 143 million smart phones in the U.S. and 71 million tablets. Ignoring mobile is no longer an option for a tactical digital team.

With a startling 81% of all millennials owning a mobile phone, clearly, if you want to reach the age group 25–34, you should consider marketing with mobile. Trends indicate that in the future, the ad campaigns that make the most impact will use a combination of media and mobile technology to bridge the gap between the real world and the online world.

---

95   Danyl Bosomworth, Mobile Marketing Statistics 2014, http://www.smartinsights.com/mobile-marketing/mobile-marketing-analytics/mobile-marketing-statistics/

96   Heidi Cohen, 67 Mobile Facts to Develop Your 2014 Budget, http://heidicohen.com/67-mobile-facts-from-2013-research-charts/

Porsche,[97] for example, used augmented reality to create an immersive experience for their consumers via a mobile app. You can hover an iPad over a Porsche, and the app will synchronize with it and display vehicle stats, details, and other extras. This is real world marketing done in a way that actively gets the consumer involved and ready to buy.

Your consumers have their mobile devices on them at all times. You can use this amazing tool—combined with mobile app technology—to deliver experiences that will blow your consumers' minds. That is how you eventually get those top conversion numbers.

Mobile marketing has arrived, and it is here to make your life easier. With so much competition, it is great to know that a well thought-out mobile strategy can still have a serious impact on your target audience.

---

97   Joe McCarthy, Porsche Looks to Augmented Reality for Immersive Panamera Experience, http://www.luxurydaily.com/porsche-looks-to-augmented-reality-for-immersive-panamera-experience/

CHAPTER 15

Native Advertising and Remarketing Vehicles

"Content that, in appearance, is native to, aka in context with, the experience of the platform, but is in reality paid placement. (You see that? It doesn't look like an ad, it looks like any of the other content except that the relationship is transparently identified.)"

MONICA BUSSOLATI

n this chapter, we will review the merits of native advertising and how remarketing can help you sell more cars to more people in less time. Your digital strategy team needs to realize that any edge in this highly competitive automotive field is a gift.

What Is Native Advertising and Remarketing?

Native advertising has been confusing entry-level digital marketing teams in the automotive industry since the term was first uttered several years ago. Only recently has it been more clearly defined so that it can be properly used by ambitious teams looking for something new to try out to get better conversions.

The definition of native advertising is "a form of media that is built into the actual visual design and where the ads are part of the content."[98] Some experts say that native advertising is the same as content marketing; others say that it is a type of content marketing that uses paid media instead of owned or earned media.

For your team, a native advert could be something as simple as an advertorial that appears on one of your leading brand's blogs or on a large car blog. Another example could be a sponsored post on Facebook or a paid tweet carrying your brand message.

Remarketing as a term gets its roots from Google. When you need to convert visitors into buyers, often one visit is not enough. Remarketing is a way of segmenting your audience of past site visitors so that you can deliver ads and display campaigns based on the actions that these individuals have taken on your site.

Remarketing can also refer to the strategies and techniques that your team uses to follow up with past website visitors that have not followed your desired course of action. A great example of remarketing in our online dealer marketing world is a potential lead arriving on one of your website landing pages then browsing around to other pages and leaving without filling out any inquiry form, contact us, or similar.

As they leave, because your website captures their cookies, Google will showcase your website ads to them to get them back to your website. These will display on other websites[99] that are part of the Google ad network. It is a method that can be used to keep your brand in front of the eyes of your target audience for as long as possible until a desired conversion happens.

They might return from a completely different website, where they spotted your ad again. Strong branding, clever ads,

---

98   Todd Wasserman, What Is 'Native Advertising'? Depends Who You Ask, http://mashable.com/2012/09/25/native-advertising/

99   What Is Retargeting and How Does It Work, https://retargeter.com/what-is-retargeting-and-how-does-it-work

and excellent conversion tactics on your website pages will help convert large portions of this lost traffic when they return.

Creating Ads That Work

Native ads[100] are being called the holy grail of digital publishing. But many digital marketing teams are still wary of it and claim that native advertising is simply a term that has replaced "sponsored content"—something that consumers despise. Imagine reading a great informative article on burgers done right online only to discover it has been sponsored by McDonalds.

It would not be so bad if the content was about something other than eating right. You can see how these would make a consumer angry. Digital strategy purists argue that native ads are different and that they are based on the principles of marketing with content. Here are some methods of using native ads that will work.

- For advertorials, do not place the terms "sponsored content" above your article. This is not native advertising, because it is fake advertising content masquerading as real content. Native ads are proud to be advertising, and they use creativity to offset that it comes from a paid source or brand.

- A new kind of sponsored content is being called branded content. This type of native advertising involves a brand-sponsored article that clearly confesses to being from that brand. Dell sponsored a post in the *New York Times*, and you could see immediately who the post was from—"Paid for and posted by Dell," along with large Dell avatars, an

---

100   Lucia Moses, Do Native Ads Work? Survey Asks Consumers What They Think of the Format, http://www.adweek.com/news/advertising-branding/do-native-ads-work-144990

inclusion in the URL stating "paidpost," and no outright calls to action.

- Product placement has long been considered a bad practice, but repackaged as native advertising using modern principles, it can be inspiring. A great example is Audible sponsoring Anna Akana's (a YouTube personality) YouTube videos—and she makes it fun by reciting the ad text on camera in different accents.

- Facebook-sponsored posts allow you to take your best Facebook update that already contains lots of influential engagement and use it as a site-wide advert that you can train on specific target demographics. This is a great example of native advertising that thinks outside the box on the social networking website.

- A paid tweet is another great example. If you have had some amazing feedback from a tweet that your brand or auto dealership has posted, why not use it as an ad? These are clearly marketed on the site and inspire lots of engagement.

Native adverts will work as long as they adhere to the editorial guidelines of the brand in question and they meet your audience's expectations. While some experts say that sites like Facebook and Twitter cannot contain native advertising, it really depends on whether the context displayed is a part of unique and informative content.

YouTube video ads that appear to be normal content are also great native ads. Some of the best video ads contain absolutely no call to action at all. They simply have a story, share a message, and then show a brief brand logo. When brands do not try to be pushy, people respond by naturally wanting to find out more.

You and your team have to practice to get native ads right because they do drive dangerously close to the much-despised sponsored posts of yesterday. Keep your plan in hand and your methods an ongoing test, and you should be fine.

Building a Complete Branding Strategy

If you are going to use native advertising extensively in your campaigns, you will have to make sure that you build a complete branding strategy first. The reason is simple: if your branding is bold and powerful, people will recognize it and understand that an advertorial is in fact an advertorial. If your branding is unclear, they may feel misled on discovery of this.

A clear and concise branding strategy[101] can be defined as the plan or motivations that lead you to create a brand identity and vision that is in line with your company culture. Your brand is not defined by the cars that you sell, the website that you have, or the team that you have put together.

It is based on the message or feeling that you want to communicate with your consumers. We also know about the USP, or Unique Selling Proposition. A great branding strategy ensures that your message is communicated consistently across any of your native ads, whether they are on a major website or on Facebook. Your brand message should always connect emotionally with your consumers and inspire them to be a part of your community.

This is achieved by sharing common ideals with your consumers and reminding them that there are human faces behind the brand in question. We are all just people selling ethically and communicating with other good people. Some of the best native ads are consumer-centric, meaning that they reward your customer base for no particular reason.

If you want to be a likable brand and have people love what you

---

101   Lauren Sorenson, 7 Components That Comprise a Comprehensive Brand Strategy, http://blog.hubspot.com/blog/tabid/6307/bid/31739/7-Components-That-Comprise-a-Comprehensive-Brand-Strategy.aspx

do, then you need to invest in rewarding your fans and consumers for caring. This will naturally cultivate loyalty among your communities instead of animosity (which is what often comes with sponsored posts). Your branding strategy has to be spot on to measure all of your decisions to make sure that they are working within the contexts you have chosen.

Always keep an eye on your return on investment when putting out native ads that are a part of your branding strategy. Just by measuring them and the installation of an A/B testing process, you will get a good sense of how your consumers feel about your actions. If advertorials do not convert, then there is no point doing them. The same goes for any other form of native ad you post.

Focus on using great, unique, and literally *your* content to define your brand, and do not be afraid to share that content—keeping it as unbiased as you can. The best native ads never contain calls to action, and they are not blatant about promoting their brand. They simply provide great, valuable content for their valued consumers with the hope that the consumer—of their own volition—will respond in kind. That is what makes true native advertising so effective.

Complete your brand strategy first before you invest in any native advertising. That way you will be able to keep the lines clear. Differentiate your automotive brand, but never stoop to tricking people.

Trends and Stats in Native Advertising and Remarketing

There is no doubt in my mind that native advertising and remarketing both have a place in your digital strategy. As an organized team that is ready for battle, these methods will add to your arsenal when you need it most. Here are some great trends and stats on the latest native advertising and remarketing methods.

- Some 70% of individuals[102] want to learn about products through content rather than through traditional advertising methods. This makes native ads desirable!

- According to Dedicated Media, people view native ads 53% more often than banner ads, and it also increases brand lift by 82%.[103]

- Seventy-one percent of publishers receive no major complaints from readers about native ad features, while 29% of them only receive minor backlash. In other words, consumers will not mind as long as you take responsibility for providing the public with quality, unbiased information that enhances (not promotes) your brand.

- Almost three quarters of polled U.S. publishers[104] have admitted to offering native advertising on their websites. Only 10% of these people did not have any plans to make native advertising a fixture on their sites.

- Some 57% of publishers are using content metrics—like engagement and time spent—as key indicators for native ads. They monitor consumer sentiment to see if anyone really takes offense to a brand having a voice about their own product.

- Remarketing from Google has been proven to work by leading SEO specialists in the field, like MOZ for example. The Google Display Network is one of the largest remarketing

---

102   Danny Wong, 11 Surprising Stats That Demonstrate Native Advertising's Value to Marketers, http://www.huffingtonpost.com/danny-wong/11-surprising-stats-that-_b_5267424.html

103   The Power of Native Advertising, http://www.dedicatedmedia.com/articles/the-power-of-native-advertising

104   Giselle Abramovich, 15 Mind-Blowing Stats About Native Advertising, http://www.cmo.com/articles/2013/10/21/15_Stats_Native_Advertising.html

networks in the world. Plus, it includes Admob for mobile targeting![105]

- RobotLizard reports that it cost them $2.86 to land a remarketing sale with an absolutely astounding 37% conversion rate.[106]

With remarketing, your digital strategy can reformulate your opinions on "the ones that get away" by bringing them back. This type of re-engagement gives you a second chance to make a first impression, and that is rare with marketing online. The key is your branding consistency! You want your consumer to know your ad is following them around.

You want it to call out to them and help you recoup some lost revenue from your other digital marketing strategies. In the automotive industry, people often return to your websites to look at cars they want or like. The more they return, the better chance you have of getting them on your email list or scheduling a test drive with them.

What Is New in the World of Remarketing?

There are a lot of dealerships that still do not know about remarketing or following your car shopper along their consumer journey or selection and buying process. It gives your brand the edge when they click through your website and deep pages and then suddenly leave. If you employ remarketing techniques, on each website they browse after yours, your amazingly effective advert will appear, calling them back. It is an excellent way to make the most of lost conversions and tell your potential customers,

---

105   Larry Kim, Remarketing: How to Make Your Content Marketing and SEO up to 7x More Awesome, http://moz.com/blog/remarketing-how-to-make-your-content-marketing-seo-up-to-7x-more-awesome

106   How Remarketing Rocks – See Real Statistics, http://www.robolizard.com/online-google-ppc-advertising-north-scottsdale-az/amazing-remarketing-statistics/

"Hey, we noticed you liked the VW Jetta; here is just a reminder that this car leases right now for just $159."

Lead conversion is a highly competitive game, as I have mentioned more than once in this field guide to digital marketing for your brand and dealership. While remarketing remains fairly new to untested digital apprentices or those new in the jobs of Internet sales and marketing managers, it is also being used incorrectly by many others. This is why it is so important to have a unified digital strategy with branding messages that work.

If you are going to waste your time with inconsistent branding, your conversions will decrease because your consumer will not recognize your message, and therefore click through rates may be lower. The few that do click because your ad is decent anyway will not understand why they have landed on your website again, and they will exit immediately.

You have to test the consumer path from your website to other sites and back to your website. If you have the resources, you can even make sure that your ad returns them to a page that they were interested in or a particularly strong landing page depending on your marketing goals and objectives.

The only new thing about remarketing since 2011 is a digital strategist's ability to use it correctly and in innovative ways. This reflects the real mettle of your team. If you can remarket to improve your landing page conversions, you can save yourself a lot of time and effort with other campaigns that cost more money.

Consider the content of the advert,[107] and try to be as friendly, likable, and alluring as you can be. Think outside the box. Most car ads show the car and a line of text—do something different! Communicate that sincere brand message or feeling with your adverts instead.

---

107   Target the Right Customers and Get More Conversions With Remarketing, http://www.autofusion.com/news/article/target-the-right-customers-and-get-more-conversions-with-remarketing

The best online marketing dealers are cashing in on lost coupon sign-ups by getting traffic to return to abandoned inquiry landing pages. You can also decide to personalize the ad experience by bringing your consumer back to a page they spent the most time on. They most likely were looking at a certain model of car that they want, so leading them back to the page of the prior desired model or service increases the changes of conversion in the form of filling out a "contact us" form or, even better, a phone call to the sales department. You can never be sure, but remarketing makes doubly sure just in case. Use it to enhance your perceived presence and branding message online and to impress car buyers by making your get-in-contact processes easy and accommodating. There is nothing better than a non-pushy ad campaign that works.

Remarketing Success Stories

Because Google leads the charge with remarketing, there are many success stories available that prove the viability of this marketing practice. While other remarketing ad networks exist, Google has over two million sites that participate, which makes following your prospect around a whole lot easier. Here are two great success stories.

InterContinental Hotels is a large hotel company with 650,000 guest rooms in more than 100 countries. The brand began with basic Google Adwords, then as they realized how many leads they were losing, decided to set a new batch of goals. They wanted to target users that had visited a hotel website without booking a stay.

They also wanted to make sure that Google's network was the best choice for them as they needed to expand their global reach. The company began using remarketing by importing existing remarketing lists into AdWords. They segmented these global campaigns by language and hotel brand; then they tested the ads' performance on multiple levels.

The results were clear to say the least. Their click through rate increased by 55%[108] after adding text ads to their campaign. They also discovered that the Google remarketing ad network was 21% more efficient at delivering leads than other networks.

HungryFish Media is another remarketing success story with a focus on the fitness and health niches. They needed to increase reach to get their ads seen more online, and they needed to boost their conversions to get more health and fitness products sold. They achieved this by using placement targeting to run ads on 2,500 large sites.

They tagged visitors with a remarketing pixel if they visited their shopping page and remarketed to them for 30 days afterwards. This incredible remarketing campaign on the Google Network resulted in an increased reach of 584%[109] compared to other ad networks and a conversion increase of 563% overall.

There are so many sites and brands that are benefitting from remarketing—booking.com, Karen Miller, Specsavers, and Confused.com. All of these websites are bringing their leads back for another shot at a conversion.

With a quality branding strategy and a team that understands how to run the best native ad campaigns in your area—coupled with remarketing—you are looking at one solid, integrated ad campaign before you have even spoken about any other major forms of advertising. I strongly suggest you incorporate these into your strategies to see the benefits for yourself.

---

108   InterContinental Hotels Group Expands Global Reach and Increases Clickthroughs With Remarketing, https://docs.google.com/a/google.com/viewer?url=http%3A%2F%2Fwww.google.com%2Fadwords%2Fdisplaynetwork%2Fpdfs%2FGDN_Case_Study_IHG.pdf

109   Hungry Fish Media Uses Remarketing to Increase Reach by 584% and Increase Conversions by 563%, https://docs.google.com/a/google.com/viewer?url=http%3A%2F%2Fwww.google.com%2Fads%2Fdisplaynetwork%2Fpdfs%2FGDN_Case_Study_HungryFishMedia.pdf&embedded=true

CHAPTER 16

Developing Long-Term Processes and Systems

"We shall defend our island, whatever the cost may be, we shall fight on the beaches, we shall fight on the landing grounds, we shall fight in the fields and in the streets, we shall fight in the hills; we shall never surrender."

WINSTON CHURCHILL

ou have reached the final chapter in this training manual, and now there is nothing left to learn other than how to develop long-term processes and systems for your brand. This is perhaps the most essential role that you will play as their digital leader.

People come and go, but brand knowledge remains. That means that you have to train your team to not only get into the habit of testing things but to learn to record their observations and results for any new team members to pick up where they left off.

Your Marketing Plan Integration

Right now your dealership has their own methods of traditional marketing that will need to be integrated with yours. You may have to start small by running minor ad campaigns and proving yourself worthy of an actual increased marketing budget by reallocating your current offline budget into online budgets. This is something that all online marketers go through. It is like earning your chops on the field of battle.

A marketing plan will help you get to this final point, where you can start being more creative with your content, your ads, and your integrated campaigns in general. An integrated marketing plan consists of a variety of different marketing methods and disciplines. All of your tactics working together for the benefit of your brand's and dealership's conversions—that is what it eventually boils down to.

A decent marketing plan combines a number of different areas, including your various research results, a digital marketing strategy, PR, direct marketing, promotions, event marketing, content marketing, print, Internet marketing and advertising, and broadcast media. These can all be governed under an integrated digital media plan.[110]

These elements will be broken down into their working parts and involve everything from your website strategy to TV, radio, print, and digital advertising and online marketing collateral, email marketing, and trade show appearances. Everything can be integrated and used to generate valuable content for your digital channels.

Once you have threshed out the outline or framework of your integrated marketing plan, you can focus on what it is going to cost to implement or conduct any or all of the proposed campaigns that are potentially viable. Remember your approach, your weapon selection, and your vehicle choices? These military tips will take you far in digital strategy.

---

110   Creating an Integrated Marketing Communications Plan, http://www.rd-marketing.com/communications-plans.htm

Website and Event Marketing Integration

Your website is the virtual face of your dealership or brand online, so it needs to be a big part of your integrated marketing plan. Along with your website, your event marketing also needs to be particularly good in the automotive niche.

As a digital dealership you will have plenty of opportunities to host, sponsor, or present an event that will inspire lots of campaigns and media creation. These need to be closely tied to your website so that you can leverage the traffic and conversions at the event on the day.

Event marketing helps you stand out from the competition by advancing your brand story and sharing your culture with your communities and consumers. Strategic combinations of online and offline marketing usually produce the best and most consistent results.

According to Marketo, 29.2%[111] of the average marketing budget is spent on digital marketing, while only 1/5 of a brand's marketing budget is spent on events. It is at events that consumers get to really experience what your dealership is all about if you do it correctly.

Online events like live streaming can inspire a lot of engagement and conversation around your brand and the campaigns that you are running. Never underestimate the power of online events to cause buzz and hype about a promotion, contest, or new car release.

Real world events like customer appreciation days, tech workshops for women, customer lunches, dog-owners Saturdays that include a free car wash and dog goodies for our four-legged friends are excellent networking opportunities, but they also give

---

111　The Definitive Guide to Event Marketing, http://www.marketo.com/definitive-guides/event-marketing/

your team a chance to collect market research and live content for your campaigns.

Use Evernote to capture photos, videos, and quotes in real time at these events, then turn them into ad campaigns and social engagements in your social platforms later on. Just do not forget to have a release form signed by the people you are taking photos of and plan to post on your social entities.

Events have an uncanny way of inspiring people to get to know who a brand and dealership really are, and that is extremely valuable for your online exposure. Do not forget that you are in the business of convincing people to buy from you and that you are the good guys, where people want to come to service their cars or buy their tires. With the integration of digital marketing and the ambition to embed the social networks in those processes, we are no longer in the Push Marketing business, which is considered to be forcing people when, what, and where to buy, but rather to pull them in when they are ready and decide from whom they want to buy what.

Be creative, and inspire a movement in your area. Do not allow your traditional marketing teams (in case you are still having marketing siloes in your organization) to stamp on yours and remove your shot at revamping how to convert leads forever.

Your customers will appreciate the battle you are fighting, and your enemies will recognize you as a formidable opponent in the digital arena with a strong team to back you up.

Regional Campaign Integration

Once you and your tactical team have spent 100 days or so perfecting your tactics and your overall plan, you can think about rolling it out on a more regional scale. Regional campaign integration is a complex pursuit with the largest rewards of all. I am talking about bigger budgets, more complex ideas, and multiple campaigns all governed under one solid plan to sell more and gain more market share.

- Make sure that your regional campaign is always consumer-centric. Everything you do and every decision that you make must be for the benefit of your consumer. Customer loyalty is important, retention is critical, and advocacy is needed. To hit on all of these points, you have to practice what you preach in digital marketing.

- Think about real world product integration with digital strategy. Ultimately, when your customer gets to your showroom floor, you want there to be a continuous experience, and completely removing the digital element reduces your opportunity to engage and sell. Invest in touch screens, augmented reality, and specialized brand experiences, just as BMW and Audi are now practicing in their new showrooms.

- Promote where your ideal customer segments hang out. This means finding out who your ideal consumers are then streamlining all marketing messages to meet these specific segments. The more specific you are, the better your chances at a sale. People will respond to what they know, believe in, and care about. Make them care.

- Practice leveraging different marketing channels, processes, and team members. Everyone and everything is flexible and should be able to change at a moment's notice for the improvement of a running campaign. On a regional scale, this can be tricky, but it can also be a very specialized skill for you to have as a digital dealer.

- Work on your regional brand identity, and make sure that everyone that works for your brand understands the culture and the objectives in mind. People should be able to recognize your logo, message, and content simply by understanding who you are.

- Continuously work on synergy or integrated marketing communications. All of your marketing tools need to be focused on a hierarchy of goals that align with your overall brand objectives and mission.
- Figure out how best to use paid, owned, and earned media and become great at content creation to leverage the various platforms that can accelerate your marketing efforts and improve your eventual return on investment.

Regional campaign integration will happen when your localized digital marketing strategies have been proven and your results have been verified. Remember that everything in digital marketing correlates with battles, from building successful, operative, and resilient teams to launching campaign attacks based on business intelligence you could gather from your competitors.

To become a master digital marketer, you also have to learn how different digital strategies exist symbiotically within a regional campaign rollout. For now, focus on the small details so that later on you will have an incredible blueprint for success. Remind yourself of Crawl – Walk – Run. First things first.

Long-term Follow Up Processes

In automotive digital marketing, your team will want to use the long-term follow up process that I have used in the past. While it is true that a majority of inbound leads (emails and phone calls) convert within 72 hours, it is also true that many more do not. If you have your prospects' email addresses, then you have to place them in a long-term follow up process.

Once they are part of your email marketing database, they are part of your process. Be careful not to send them dozens of spammy emails within the first several weeks of signing up. I personally, as an Internet Sales Manager, used a starting process with no more than three emails a week for the first two weeks and one email a month later on if they were considered as a long-term prospect. And do not forget, even though we are Internet sales people, the phone is and always will be our most important tool to convert leads into sales. When I had team members who avoided calling up the prospect, I always gave them one "VJ Wisdom" on their way, which is "You are writing for the show and phoning for the dow"...most likely they got the message.

According to a New Autoshopper.com study, automotive Internet users report that they first decide to buy a new vehicle 15.4 weeks[112] before they actually physically purchase one. Based on this data, if you believe you are making the most of your conversions, then you are wrong! Long-term process integration is not a "could do" thing but a "must have" necessity. Do it.

A long-term follow-up process will build customer satisfaction, maximize long-term sales volumes, and pick up any lost conversions that short-term digital campaigns and remarketing may have left behind or let off the hook. When you eliminate the chance of missing out on potential prospects by adopting the correct long-term email marketing practices, revenues leap ahead.

A follow up process can be defined as a system or set of systems that effectively build and enhance your relationship with a prospect to increase their engagement with your business so they become more influenced to buy from you.[113]

---

112   Adam Ross, How Much Time Do You Spend Working Your 15,30,45,60,75 and 90-Day Old Car Dealership Prospects? Probably Not Enough, http://infiniteprospects. com/digital-marketing-for-car-dealerships/automotive-internet-sales/focus-on-long-term-follow-up/

113   24 Step Follow Up Process, http://www.slideshare.net/REVSalesFCP1/24-step-follow-up-process

Stats, Facts, and Trends in Online Marketing

To complete this field guide and end your first journey into becoming a leader in your dealership's digital marketing arena, here are some of the latest stats, facts, and trends that you need to know about in online marketing today.

- Focus on big data and building a big data system for your brand so that you can begin recording, tracking, measuring, and using all of the data that your dealership generates. Then use this data to train and educate your team members and improve your consumer engagement and sales.

- Some 34 million[114] Americans plan to buy a vehicle in the next six months. One report finds that these consumers are more than twice as likely to be swayed by auto-focused digital marketing. Automotive shoppers are 71% more likely to be influenced by digital advertising than the average consumer.

- Each month there are 10.3 billion Google searches with 78% of U.S. Internet users researching products and services online (including cars).[115]

- Econsultancy reports that real-time marketing is faster than we all believed possible. The Survey Report concluded that four-fifths of all respondents said that brand responses should happen in two minutes or less.[116]

- App conversion rates are closer to desktop conversions than mobile website conversions. The difference is apps (1.8%), desktop (2.4%), and mobile site (0.73%).

---

114   15 Mind-Blowing Stats About Automotive Brands, http://www.cmo.com/articles/2014/4/7/15_stats_auto_brands.html

115   Tom Pick, 83 Exceptional Social Media and Marketing Statistics for 2014, http://www.business2community.com/social-media/83-exceptional-social-media-marketing-statistics-2014-0846364#!bg3TCN

116   David Moth, 10 interesting Digital Marketing Statistic We've Seen This Week, https://econsultancy.com/blog/64422-10-interesting-digital-marketing-statistics-we-ve-seen-this-week-20

- Google click-to-call is used by more than 40% of mobile searchers, and an astonishing 94% of smartphone users need to call the business directly when searching for information—whether click-to-call is available or not.

- With advances in hologram technology, augmented reality, and many other innovative mobile technologies, expect converged media to become the norm over the next few years. Digital dealers that learn to launch successful converged media campaigns will earn the most revenue for their brands.

Marketing online is becoming a deeply intricate field of study. The good news is that it provides real time on-the-job training for you and your team. I firmly believe in the process of planning, testing, and revamping. I hope it serves you well on the digital battlefield.

Conclusion

Digital strategy means battle. You will be fighting with your team, with your dealership's leadership team, and with your competitors. At each stage, there is a way to deal with these battles and win them one by one using the solid digital marketing practices outlined in this book.

You now understand the setup process—and the war that you face. To become the digital marketer that you were always meant to be is going to require hard work, planning, and the ability to fail gracefully, pick yourself up, and then succeed with your team.

The warzone is primed for your entry. Select your strategic digital strategy approach. Then decide on the best weapons of war. Conclude your assembly process by choosing the right vehicles for your methods and tactics to thrive on.

None of this would be possible without your crack team of specially assembled Internet sales people. They will watch for enemy fire. They will see when the opportunity rises and your team can strike. Digital dealing in the automotive field is not easy, but it does come with a lot of rewards if you put in the time.

My sincere hope is that this humble field guide to setting up your team and creating your digital campaigns will spark a flame inside you that drives you forward for many years to come. You have the power to lead your team through perilous times and through many challenges, obstacles, and hardships.

My advice is not to sit tight. The best defense is a good offense. Learn and soak in all you can; fail then fail again. Make sure that each of your team members loves what they do and cannot get enough of the results that they earn.

Choose your battles wisely, and eventually you will win your market. Your brand and car dealership will become legendary in your home town. It is up to you now.

Brothers in digital arms,

Volker Jaeckel

References

Chapter 1

Jones, Alicia, *ZMOT – The New Mental Model of Marketing*, http://www.media-mosaic.com/blog/zmot/zmot-the-new-mental-model-of-marketing/

Lecinski, Jim, *The Zero Moment Of Truth: A New Marketing Strategy*, http://adwords.blogspot.com/2011/07/zero-moment-of-truth-new-marketing.html

Dunay, Paul, *How To Make The Zero Moment Of Truth Work For You,* http://socialmediatoday.com/pauldunay/1515541/consumer-online-behavior-how-make-zero-moment-truth-work-you

Zero Moment Of Truth (ZMOT), http://www.google.com.au/think/collections/zero-moment-truth.html

Shaw, Colin, *15 Statistics That Should Change The Business World – But Haven't,* http://www.linkedin.com/today/post/article/20130604134550-284615-15-statistics-that-should-change-the-business-world-but-haven-t

The Customer Journey To Online Purchases, http://www. thinkwithgoogle.com/tools/customer-journey-to-online-purchase.html

The Aero Moment Of Truth For Automotive Study, http://www. thinkwithgoogle.com/research-studies/zmot-auto-study.html

Chapter 2

Arling-Giorgi, Alison, *For Gen Y, Brands Are Our Peers*, http://www. pbs.org/wgbh/pages/frontline/media/generation-like/allison-arling-giorgi-for-gen-y-brands-are-our-peers/

Gen Z Shopping: Designing Retail For The Constant State Of Partial Attention, http://www.fitch.com/content/uploads/2013/09/GenZshopping_09_09_13_final.pdf

Archer, Jeffrey, *Gen Z Prefer Practical Cars*, http://www.autotrader. com/research/article/car-news/109798/gen-x-prefers-practical-cars.jsp

Mc Millan, John, *The Importance Of Market Segments*, http://www. mcmillantech.co.uk/articles/MarketSegments.pdf

Garrison, Lyndsay, *The Importance Of Customer Segmentation*, http:// www.yourcrmteam.com/blog/2011/08/the-importance-of-customer-segmentation/

Silk Carty, Sharon, *Auto Sales, Driven By Boomers, Automakers Desperate For Millennial Love*, http://www.huffingtonpost. com/2012/05/04/baby-boomers-driving-cars_n_1475243.html

Naughton, Keith, *Boomers Replace Their Children As No. 1 Market For Autos*, http://www.bloomberg.com/news/2013-08-05/automania-strikes-boomers-supplanting-kids-as-buyers.html

Neeser, Shannon, *The Unsung Generation: How Xers Add Value To Your Association*, http://xyzuniversity.com/2014/01/the-unsung-generation-how-xers-add-value-to-your-association/

Next Generation Car Buyer Study, http://www.autonews.com/assets/PDF/CA90353823.PDF

Sladek, Sarah, *Why Gen Won't Buy What You're Selling*, http:// xyzuniversity.com/2012/10/why-gen-y-wont-buy-what-youre-selling/

Pitts, Anna, *How To Network With Generation Y,* http://xyzuniversity.com/2014/04/how-to-network-with-generation-y/

Gen Z Has Arrived: Get To Know Them, http://xyzuniversity.com/2014/03/gen-z-has-arrived-get-to-know-them/

Chapter 3

Handrick, Jeremiah, *What Makes For A Great Digital Strategist,* http://jeremiahandrick.com/notes/2012/03/19/what-makes-for-a-great-digital-strategist

Patel, Nish, *The Hierarchy Of Work-In-Progress Strategies,* http://www.conceptshare.com/2014/04/the-hierarchy-of-work-in-progress-strategies/

Humphrey, Stephen, E, Hollenbeck, John, R, Meyer, Christopher, J, Ilgen, Daniel, R, *Hierarchical Team Decision Making,* http://www.emeraldinsight.com/books.htm?chapterid=1781313

Perlstein, Tim, Fenton, Bethany, *Organizing For Digital Success,* http://razorfishoutlook.razorfish.com/articles/organizingdigital.aspx#01

Adapting To A Networked World, http://communicopia.com/insights/digital-teams

Non-Profit Digital Teams Report – Influence And Impact, http://digitalteams.org/

Shaw, Amanda, *How to Take Control Of Your Digital Marketing,* http://webrunnermedia.com/control-your-digital-marketing/

Hamilton, Chris, *B2B Marketing Strategy: Take Control Of Your Teams With A Sales And Marketing Service Level Agreement,* http://blog.stargazerdigital.co.uk/use-sales-marketing-agreement-take-control-b2b-marketing-strategy

Modeling The Experience Cycle, https://interactions.acm.org/archive/view/may-june-2008/on-modelingthe-experience-cycle1

Clong, Mary, *When It's Time To Hire A Digital Strategist Beware Of Social Charlatans,* http://socialmediatoday.com/maryclong/1674301/

when-its-time-hire-digital-strategist-beware-social-charlatans

Hollis Thomases, Augustine, Fou, Dr, *Questions You Should Ask When Hiring A "Digital Strategist"*, http://www.slideshare.net/HollisThomases/qs-to-ask-when-hiring-digital-strategist

Training Tips From The Classroom Building Stronger Digital Advertising Sales Teams, http://www.digitalstrategyconsulting.com/insight/DIR_Training_tips_from_the_classroom-DMSA.pdf

Hewitt, Perry, *How To Build A High Perfoming Digital Team*, http://blogs.hbr.org/2013/08/how-to-build-a-high-performing/

Chapter 4

Tzu, Sun, The Art Of War Quotes, http://www.goodreads.com/work/quotes/3200649—s-nz-b-ngf

Analysts Say Digital Strategy Management Is Critical To Success, http://aptris.com/news-events/itsm-insights/itsm/analysts-say-digital-strategy-management-is-critical-to-success/

Digital Marketing Blocked By Skills And Time In Brand Teams, http://www.digitalstrategyconsulting.com/intelligence/2014/02/most_digital_marketers_expect_a_single_view_of_the_customer_by_2016_infographic.php

Krill, Paul, *Forrester: Businesses Having Trouble Getting With The Digital Times*, http://www.infoworld.com/t/it-strategy/forrester-businesses-having-trouble-getting-the-digital-times-241997

Michiels, Ian, *The Marketers Guide To Justifying Investments In Digital Asset Management*, http://www.saepio.com/workspace/media/misc/Marketers%20Guide%20to%20Justifying%20DAM%20Investments.pdf

Winter, Brian, *Digital Marketing*, http://www.slideshare.net/CarpathiaHosting/digital-marketing-how-to-justify-investments-quantify-returns

Parker, Steve, Jr, *Lack Of Digital Strategy & Accountability Is Killing Brands*, http://blogs.imediaconnection.com/blog/2012/03/01/lack-of-digital-strategy-accountability-is-killing-brands/

Vinton, Merici, Keane, Michael, *Better Accountability Through Open Data,* http://strataconf.com/stratany2014/public/schedule/detail/36469

Chapter 5

Quotes About Strategy, http://www.goodreads.com/quotes/tag/strategy

Borges, Bernie, *4 Elements Pf A Digital Marketing Roadmap,* http://www.findandconvert.com/2012/10/4-elements-of-a-digital-marketing-roadmap/

Wang, Ray, *Why Every Company Needs To Build A Digital Roadmap,* http://www.smartt.com/insights/why-every-company-needs-build-digital-roadmap

Bennett, Shea, *Web, Mobile, Email, Apps, Social Media – Your Digital Marketing Road Map (Infographic),* http://www.mediabistro.com/alltwitter/digital-marketing-roadmap_b56773

Chapter 6

Lewan, Eric, *Military Quotes,* http://www.oocities.org/heratyk/milquote3.html

Brand Strategy Roadmap – Be Irresistible To Your Customers, http://www.smartt.com/branding/strategy

Building A Strategic Cross-Channel Roadmap, http://www.experian.com/assets/marketing-services/white-papers/cross-channel-roadmap-digital.pdf

Crouch, Taylor, *Consistency And Creativity In Digital Strategy,* http://enveritasgroup.com/2013/12/27/consistency-creativity-digital-strategy/

Merhige, Monique, *Consistency Is Key In Your Integrated Marketing Strategy,* http://digitalethos.org/consistency-is-key-in-your-integrated-marketing-strategy/

Danielle, *Why You Need A Follow Up Sales Strategy,* http://tresnicmedia.com/why-you-need-a-follow-up-sales-strategy/

Mapping Marketing Processes For Automation – Save Time And Increase Efficiency, http://www.pardot.com/webinars/recorded-webinar-mapping-marketing-processes-automation/

Brinker, Scott, *Gartner's Mind-Blowing Digital Marketing Transit Map,* http://chiefmartec.com/2013/06/gartners-mind-blowing-digital-marketing-transit-map/

4 Steps To Map A Digital Strategy, http://bigthunk.com/articles/4-steps-to-map-a-digital-strategy/

Digital Strategy And Vision Planning, http://www.pblasio.com/services/servicesdigital-strategy-and-vision-planning/

Flying-By-The-Seat-Of-Your-Pants As a Digital Strategy, http://www.australianbusiness.com.au/marketing/resources/flying-by-the-seat-of-your-pants-as-a-digital-stra

Chapter 7

Competition Quotes, http://www.brainyquote.com/quotes/keywords/competition.html

SWOT Analysis – A Key Competitive Intelligence Too, http://ci4winstrategy.com/uploads/SWOTAnalysis.pdf

Rae, Lisa, *Evaluating Your Competition,* http://www.internetmarketingpress.com/marketing/evaluating-your-competition/

Paglia, Ralph, *Car Dealers Must Monitor The Social Web To Remain Competitive,* http://www.dealermarketing.com/internet-marketing/social-media/3037-car-dealers-must-monitor-the-social-web-to-remain-competitive

Tougher Competition, Healthier Auto Industry, http://www.thestar.com.my/Business/Business-News/2014/01/25/Tougher-competition-healthier-industry-The-National-Automotive-Policy-NAP-is-crafted-to-liberalise-a/

Competitive Intelligence, http://www.entrepreneur.com/encyclopedia/competitive-intelligence

Helm, Burt, *How To Use Competitive Intelligence To Gain An Advantage,* http://www.inc.com/magazine/20110401/how-to-use-competitive-intelligence-to-gain-an-advantage.html

Elder, Allan, *5 Targets Of Competitive Attack On Your Business,* http://biznik.com/articles/five-targets-of-competitive-attack-on-your-business

Marketing Warfare Strategies, http://en.wikipedia.org/wiki/Marketing_warfare_strategies

Klie, Leonard, *Stress Test Customer Service With Mystery Shopping,* http://www.destinationcrm.com/Articles/Editorial/Magazine-Features/Stress-Test-Customer-Service-with-Mystery-Shopping-88908.aspx

Larranaga, Jim, *Mystery Shopping Gains Momentum In The Digital Age,* http://www.bluespiremarketing.com/blog/March-2013/mystery-shopping-gains-momentum-in-the-digital-age

Trout, Jack, *Brand Strategy: Set Up A Positive And Attack,* http://www.brandingstrategyinsider.com/2012/05/brand-strategy-set-up-a-positive-and-attack.html#.U8PX5PmSySo

Social Media Marketing, *Car Dealer Internet Battle Plan Strategy – Content, Impressions, Traffic, Interaction, Process And Sales,* http://www.slideshare.net/ADPSocialMediaMarketing/car-dealer-internet-battle-plan-strategy-content-impressions-traffic-interaction-process-and-sales

Chapter 8

Competition Quotes, http://www.brainyquote.com/quotes/keywords/competition.html

Manker, Ashley, D, *What Is Guerilla Marketing? – Definition, Strategies & Examples,* http://education-portal.com/academy/lesson/what-is-guerrilla-marketing-definition-strategies-examples.html#lesson

Lum, Ryan, *Top Car Guerilla Marketing Examples,* http://www.creativeguerrillamarketing.com/guerrilla-marketing/top-car-guerrilla-marketing-examples/

Winter, Ezra, *Who's Driving You? Smear Campaigns Go Digital: Uber Under Fire,* http://whatweekly.com/2014/06/04/whos-driving-you-case-study/

Crama, Lars, *Bridging The Gap Between CRM And Digital Marketing – In 5 Steps,* http://www.slideshare.net/larscrama/bridging-the-gap-between-crm-and-digital-marketing

Hannaford, Alley, CRM And Its Impacts On Digital Marketing, http://creative-jar.com/insights/publications/digital-marketing/crm-and-its-impacts-on-digital-marketing/

Paglia, Ralph, *Research Study Shows Online Video Advertising Is 200 Percent More Effectice Than TV,* http://www.automotivedigitalmarketing.com/profiles/blogs/research-study-shows-online-video-advertising-is-200-percent-more

De Marco, Tara, *The First 6 Steps To Successful Converged Media (Paid, Owned, And Earned),* http://blog.bazaarvoice.com/2012/10/03/the-first-6-steps-to-successful-converged-media-paid-owned-and-earned/

Slegg, Jennifer, *Creating Campaigns That Count: The Impact Of Converged Media #SESCHI,* http://www.clickz.com/clickz/news/2305441/creating-campaigns-that-count-the-impact-of-converged-media-seschi

Chapter 9

50 Inspirational Marketing Quotes: 2013, http://blog.wishpond.com/post/70494294231/50-inspirational-marketing-quotes-2013

Evans, Dean, *Internet Lead Aggregators: Be Everywhere On The Web For $200 Per Vehicle,* http://www.dealermarketing.com/internet-marketing/online-marketing/472-internet-lead-aggregators-be-everywhere-on-the-web-for-200-per-vehicle

How Retargeting Works, https://www.adroll.com/retargeting

SEO, The Bedrock Of Online Marketing, http://www.gforces.co.uk/total-digital-marketing/view/364/seo

Edwards, Victoria, *SEO Basics: 8 Essentials When Optimizing Your Site,* http://searchenginewatch.com/article/2259693/SEO-Basics-8-Essentials-When-Optimizing-Your-Site

Native Advertising, http://www.sharethrough.com/nativeadvertising/'

Wegert, Tess, *The Next Iteration Of Native Advertising Will Be Interactive,* http://www.clickz.com/clickz/column/2301114/the-next-iteration-of-native-advertising-will-be-interactive'

Digital Ad Spending In US Auto Industry Racing Ahead, http://www.emarketer.com/Article/Digital-Ad-Spending-US-Auto-Industry-Racing-Ahead/1010872

Hallett, Tony, *What Is Native Advertising Anyway?* http://www.theguardian.com/media-network-outbrain-partner-zone/native-advertising-quality-scalability

Okpagu, Ifesinachi, *Combining Online, Offline Marketing Tactics For Optimal Results,* http://www.punchng.com/i-punch/combining-online-offline-marketing-tactics-for-optimal-results/

Kehrberg, Shaun, *How To Score Before And After The Big Game,* http://www.automotivedigitalmarketing.com/profiles/blogs/how-to-score-before-and-after-the-big-game

Pritchard, David, *The Three Phases Of Digital Dealership Digital Marketing,* http://www.autodealermonthly.com/channel/dps-office/article/story/2011/08/the-three-phases-of-dealership-digital-marketing.aspx

K'string, Jan-Christoph, *Eight Trends Shaping Digital Marketing In The Auto Industry,* http://www.mckinsey.com/client_service/marketing_and_sales/latest_thinking/eight_trends_shaping_digital_marketing_in_the_auto_industry

Chapter 10

28 Stimulating Digital And Social Media Marketing Quotes, http://www.fuelingnewbusiness.com/2011/02/23/28-stimulating-digital-and-social-media-marketing-quotes/

Revving Up Automotive Digital Marketing ROI, http://www.accenture.com/SiteCollectionDocuments/PDF/Accenture-Revving-Up-Automotive-Digital-Marketing-ROI.pdf

Bendrick, Klas, *Using IT As A Competitive Advantage,* http://automotive.cioreview.com/cioviewpoint/using-it-as-a-competitive-advantage--nid-984-cid-4.html

Mayland, Bjoern, Heiland, Thomas, Dr, *Managing Variety On The Internet – Strategic Competitive Advantage In the Automotive*

Industry, http://www.wirtschaft.fh-dortmund.de/~ib/DIfEaIS/HTML/ PDF/Mayland_Heiland.pdf

Alicandri, Jeremy, *The Differential Advantages That Made Cobalt The "Elephant" Of Automotive Digital Marketing,* http://www.drivingsales. com/blogs/jeremy/2013/11/13/the-differential-advantages-allowed-cobalt-to-become-elephant-automotive-digital-marketing

Farmer, David, *Measuring Success Of Your Digital Marketing Strategy,* http://www.automotivedigitalmarketing.com/profiles/blogs/ measuring-success-of-your-digital-marketing-strategy

Chapter 11

Nelson, Amanda, *40 Inspiring Marketing Quotes From SEO Experts,* http://www.exacttarget.com/blog/40-inspiring-marketing-quotes-from-seo-experts/

Sprung, Rachel, *Pandas, Penguins, Hummingbirds, Oh My! How To Keep Up With The Latest SEO Trends,* http://blog.hubspot.com/ marketing/how-to-keep-up-seo-trends-ht

Haynes, Marie, *Your Google Algorithm Cheat Sheet: Panda, Penguin, And Hummingbird,* http://moz.com/blog/google-algorithm-cheat-sheet-panda-penguin-hummingbird

Slegg, Jennifer, *Matt Cutts: Write Clear, Understandable Content,* http://searchenginewatch.com/article/2331473/Matt-Cutts-Write-Clear-Understandable-Content

Slegg, Jennifer, *Matt Cutts Talks SEO For Google: 9 Things You Should Expect This Summer,* http://searchenginewatch.com/article/2267962/ Matt-Cutts-Talks-SEO-for-Google-9-Things-You-Should-Expect-This-Summer

Nimetz, Jody, *Google May 2014 Algorithm Updates,* http://blog. mediative.com/en/2014/05/29/google-may-2014-algorithm-updates/'

Goins, Jeff, *The Surprising Key To Becoming An Authority,* http:// goinswriter.com/authority-blog/

Alexis, Michael, *Ana Hoffman's Six Steps To Becoming An Authority Blogger,* http://www.biggirlbranding.com/ana-hoffmans-six-steps-to-becoming-an-authority-blogger/

La Barbera, Vinny, *25 Ways To Build Online Authority,* http://www.imforza.com/blog/25-ways-to-build-online-authority/

Content Marketing Infographic Of The week: Visual Storytelling, http://www.wolfgangdigital.com/blog/content-marketing/content-marketing-infographic-week-visual-storytelling/

McCale, Christina, *Four Tactics to Curate Content The Right Way,* http://www.elto.com/blog/four-tactics-to-curate-content-the-right-way/

Owens, Lauren, *The Elements Of Good Storytelling & How You Can Use Storytelling In Marketing,* http://www.morevisibility.com/blogs/seo/the-elements-of-good-storytelling-how-you-can-use-storytelling-in-marketing.html

Chapter 12

101 Shocking Helpful Online Marketing Quotes, http://www.blog-growth.com/101-shocking-helpful-quotes-for-online-marketing-from-the-bests/

Beerworth, Robert, *Do Bigger Images Mean Better Conversion Rates?* http://www.wiliam.com.au/wiliam-blog/web-design-sydney-do-bigger-images-mean-better-conversion-rates-

How Hyundai Increased Requests For Test Drive By 62% Using Multivariate Testing, https://vwo.com/blog/multivariate-testing-case-study/

How Do Colors Affect Purchases? http://blog.kissmetrics.com/color-psychology/

Lister, Jonathan, *How Does Color Affect Advertising?* http://smallbusiness.chron.com/color-affect-advertising-30998.html

Morris. Brian. *10 Colors That Increase Sales, And Why,* http://www.business2community.com/marketing/10-colors-that-increase-sales-and-why-0366997#!bgB1gU

Potratz, Paul, *What's Your Call To Action?* http://www.automotivedigitalmarketing.com/profiles/blogs/what-s-your-call-to-action

Fitzpatrick, *Engage Consumers With Calls To Action,* http://fitzpatrickadvertising.com/engage-consumers-with-calls-to-action/

Difference Between Bounce Rate & Exit Rate, http://maxivak.com/difference-between-bounce-rate-exit-rate-google-analytics/

Kaushik, Avinash, *Standard Metrics Revisited: #3: Bounce Rate,* http://www.kaushik.net/avinash/standard-metrics-revisited-3-bounce-rate/

New Car Photos – Performance Stats And Ideas, http://www.dealerrefresh.com/photos-of-new-cars-matter/

Eye Candy ... How Stock Photos Can Kill A Vehicle's Love Life, http://www.dealerrefresh.com/stock-new-car-photos-vs-actual-photos/

Essenmacher, Kim, *Do Car Photos Really Make A Difference From Stock Photos?* http://www.automotivedigitalmarketing.com/forum/topics/do-new-car-photos-really-make-a-difference-from-stock-photos

Chapter 13

Tribes Quotes, https://www.goodreads.com/work/quotes/3873014-tribes-we-need-you-to-lead-us

Beard, Ross, *What Are Brand Advocates? Why Are They Important?,* http://blog.clientheartbeat.com/brand-advocates/

The Importance of Customer Retention and Brand Advocates, http://rewardstream.com/customer-retention-brand-advocates/

Don't Let Bad Review Slow You Down: Automotive Business and Car Dealership Review Sites To Monitor, http://www.reviewtrackers.com/dont-bad-reviews-slow-down-automotive-business-car-dealership-review-sites-monitor/

Bennet, Shea, *The Best Time To Post On Facebook, Twitter Google+, LinkedIn and Pinterest [Infographic],* http://www.mediabistro.com/alltwitter/social-best-times-post_b49546

Cooper, Belle Beth, *A Scientific Guide To Posting Tweets, Facebook Posts, Emails, and Blog Posts at The Best Time,* http://blog.bufferapp.com/best-time-to-tweet-post-to-facebook-send-emails-publish-blogposts

The Best Time of Day To Post on Instagram, http://trackmaven.com/blog/2013/09/the-best-time-of-day-to-post-on-instagram/

Jaume, Jasmine, *What Is Social Media Monitoring? Answers To Common Questions and Misconceptions,* http://www.brandwatch.com/2013/02/what-is-social-media-monitoring-answers-to-common-questions-and-misconceptions/

Benefits of Social Media Monitoring For Auto Dealers, http://www.slideshare.net/wikimotive/benefits-of-social-media-monitoring-for-auto-dealers

Chapter 14

Ratcliff, Christopher, *28 Inspiring Mobile Marketing Quotes,* https://econsultancy.com/blog/65001-28-inspiring-mobile-marketing-quotes

Steward, Patsy, *Digital Media Marketing For Auto Dealers,* http://www.slideshare.net/stewartb2b/digital-marketing-auto-dealers

Miller, Michael, *YouTube Success: Tracking Your Video Performance,* http://www.nbcnews.com/id/52400163/ns/business-small_business/t/youtube-success-tracking-your-video-performance/#.U8e-ofmSySo

Adelson-Yan, Jeff, *YouTube Trends Dashboard For Data-Driven Marketers,* http://www.askingsmarterquestions.com/youtube-trends-dashboard-for-data-driven-marketers/

Hayzlett, Jeffrey, *Why Video Marketing Is Key in 2014,* http://hayzlett.com/blog/why-video-marketing-key-2014/

Abramovich, Giselle, *15 Stats Brands Should Know About Online Video,* http://digiday.com/brands/celtra-15-must-know-stats-for-online-video/

Robertson, Mark, *Car Dealers Embrace Online Video – Automotive Online Video marketing Trends,* http://www.dealerrefresh.com/car-dealers-embrace-online-video/

Tode, Chantal, *Renault Launches Highly Targeted Mobile Campaign Targeting Electric Car Enthusiasts,* http://www.mobilemarketer.com/cms/news/advertising/17870.html

Johnson, Derek, *SMS Open Rates Exceed 99%,* http://www.tatango.com/blog/sms-open-rates-exceed-99/

Aziz, Plus, *10 Top Digital Campaigns By Auto Brands In The Creative Sandbox Archive,* http://www.psfk.com/2012/10/digital-auto-advertising-examples.html#!bgREFA

Lexus – Creating Amazing, http://www.thinkwithgoogle.com/campaigns/lexus-lexus-creating-amazing.html

Abramovich, Giselle, *15 Mind Blowing Stats About YouTube,* http://www.cmo.com/articles/2014/5/19/mind_blowing_stats_youtube.html

Chapter 15

10 Definitions of Native Advertising, http://bussolati.com/10-definitions-native-advertising/

Target The Right Customers and Get More Conversions With Remarketing, http://www.autofusion.com/news/article/target-the-right-customers-and-get-more-conversions-with-remarketing

Dolan, Sean, *29 Ways To Use Remarketing (And How To Get Started),* http://squawk.im/advertising/howto-remarketing/

Kerschbaum, Joseph, *7 Winning Strategies For PPC Remarketing Success,* http://searchenginewatch.com/article/2070630/7-Winning-Strategies-for-PPC-Remarketing-Success

Success Stories, http://www.google.com/ads/displaynetwork/success-stories.html

Case Study, https://docs.google.com/a/google.com/viewer?url=http%3A%2F%2Fwww.google.com%2Fads%2Fdisplaynetwork%2Fpdfs%2FGDN_Case_Study_HungryFishMedia.pdf&embedded=true

Noble, Samantha, *Cracking Examples of Effective Remarketing and How To Compete,* http://www.koozai.com/blog/pay-per-click-ppc/cracking-examples-of-effective-remarketing-and-how-to-compete/

How Remarketing Rocks – See Real Statistics, http://www.robolizard.com/online-google-ppc-advertising-north-scottsdale-az/amazing-remarketing-statistics/

Kilbourn, Chris, *Remarketing 101: A Beginners Guide,* http://www.searchenginejournal.com/remarketing-101-beginners-guide/89043/

Wong, Danny, *11 Surprising Stats That Demonstrate Native Advertising's Value To Marketers,* http://www.huffingtonpost.com/danny-wong/11-surprising-stats-that-_b_5267424.html

The Power of Native Advertising, http://www.dedicatedmedia.com/articles/the-power-of-native-advertising

Abramovich, Giselle, *15 Mind Blowing Stats About Native Advertising,* http://www.cmo.com/articles/2013/10/21/15_Stats_Native_Advertising.html

Kim, Larry, *Remarketing: How To Make Your Content Marketing and SEO Up To 7x More Awesome,* http://moz.com/blog/remarketing-how-to-make-your-content-marketing-seo-up-to-7x-more-awesome

Chapter 16

War Quotes, http://www.brainyquote.com/quotes/topics/topic_war.html

Chaffey, Dave, *Digital Marketing Statistics 2014,* http://www.smartinsights.com/marketplace-analysis/customer-analysis/digital-marketing-statistics-sources/

Moth, David, *10 Interesting Digital Marketing Statistics We've Seen This Week,* https://econsultancy.com/blog/64422-10-interesting-digital-marketing-statistics-we-ve-seen-this-week-20

Lee, Jessica, *70% of Consumers Researching Cars Turn To Search Engines First [Stats],* http://searchenginewatch.com/article/2340699/70-of-Consumers-Researching-Cars-Turn-to-Search-Engines-First-Stats

Abramovich, Giselle, *15 Mind Blowing Stats About Automotive Brands,* http://www.cmo.com/articles/2014/4/7/15_stats_auto_brands.html

Pick, Tom, *83 Exceptional Social Media and Marketing Statistics For 2014,* http://www.business2community.com/social-media/83-exceptional-social-media-marketing-statistics-2014-0846364#!bg3TCN

Ross, Adam, *How Much Time Do You Spend Working Your 15, 30, 45, 60, 75, and 90 Day Old Car Dealership Prospects? Probably Not Enough?,* http://infiniteprospects.com/digital-marketing-for-car-dealerships/automotive-internet-sales/focus-on-long-term-follow-up/

25 Steps Follow Up System, http://www.slideshare.net/REVSalesFCP1/24-step-follow-up-process

About the Author

Volker Jaeckel is a high-energy, results-driven, international automotive sales and marketing executive, who worked for America's #1 Digital Marketing Solutions Company and for two of the top-50 dealer groups in the automotive industry.

He has led retail sales retention strategy, business development intelligence, and digital marketing consulting for several early-stage adaptions in B2B as well as B2C relationships.

Volker's 20+ years in business includes roles as international Digital Marketing Ambassador and Visionary of Consumer Experience at ADP | Cobalt, Sales & Marketing Director for an advertising start-up, and he has served as an Ecommerce and Internet Sales Director for a $900 million automotive group.

Jaeckel provides the skills, approach, and "can-do" attitude needed to lead and plan effective multi-channel sales and marketing in the age of Automotive Online Marketing. He possesses the real world, practical skills and knowledge required to lead teams, process integration, drive change, and collaborate in the complex automotive digital marketing and media advertising environments.

As the featured cover story of Digital Dealer's 2009 magazine, Volker had already created as early as 2007 a *new* media presence for his successful operating automotive group, which automotive marketers still use today as a blueprint for social engagement. Driving Sales CEO Jared Hamilton has given outstanding praise to the strategies Volker defined in his work and named him in the Top-10 ranking Ecommerce Marketing Executives in the United States.

Made in the USA
San Bernardino, CA
22 August 2016